Accelerated Learning

18 Powerful Ways to Learn Anything Superfast! Improve Your Memory Efficiency. Think Bigger and Succeed Bigger! Great to Listen in a Car!

© **Copyright Tony Bennis 2019 - All rights reserved.**

The content contained within this book may not be reproduced, duplicated or transmitted without direct written permission from the author or the publisher.

Under no circumstances will any blame or legal responsibility be held against the publisher, or author, for any damages, reparation, or monetary loss due to the information contained within this book, either directly or indirectly.

Legal Notice:

This book is copyright protected. It is only for personal use. You cannot amend, distribute, sell, use, quote or paraphrase any part, or the content within this book, without the consent of the author or publisher.

Disclaimer Notice:

Please note the information contained within this document is for educational and entertainment purposes only. All effort has been executed to present accurate, up to date, reliable, complete information. No warranties of any kind are declared or implied. Readers acknowledge that the author is not engaging in the rendering of legal, financial, medical or professional advice. The content within this book has been derived from various sources. Please consult a licensed professional before attempting any techniques outlined in this book.

By reading this document, the reader agrees that under no circumstances is the author responsible for any losses, direct or indirect, that are incurred as a result of the use of information contained within this document, including, but not limited to, errors, omissions, or inaccuracies.

Table of Contents

Introduction..6

Chapter 1: Learning as a Lifestyle.............17

Chapter 2: DiSSS Method........................25

Chapter 3: Mixing Things Up with Interleaved Practice...................................32

Chapter 4: PACER Method........................41

Chapter 5: Mind Mapping........................47

Chapter 6: Mnemonic Devices...................53

Chapter 7: The Art of Speed Reading.........57

Chapter 8: Accelerated Learning Through Effective Note-taking...................................68

Chapter 9: Battling Procrastination to Accelerate Learning...................................75

Chapter 10: The Feynman Technique........82

Chapter 11: Learning Through Listening..88

Chapter 12: Experiential Learning............96

Chapter 13: The Method of Loci - A Memory Technique..102

Chapter 14: Efficient Cramming for an Exam...109

Chapter 15: Collaborative Learning in a Group Setting..118

Chapter 16: Binaural Beats for Effective Studying..................................*124*

Chapter 17: Flashcards for Effective Studying..................................*130*

Chapter 18: A Case for Spaced Repetition..................................*137*

Conclusion..................................*143*

References..................................*147*

Introduction

Learning is always going to be a lifelong process. As a child you are conditioned to learn the fundamental principles involved in being a functional human being. You are taught how to walk, talk, run, jump, play, count, sing, dance, etc. As you get older, learning becomes increasingly more complex and challenging. However, you also know that failing to learn means failing to adapt. That's why you keep on encouraging yourself to do it.

It's something that we have to consistently incorporate into our daily lives if we are to continually grow and develop as people. It is vital that we make it a habit to learn new things every day if we want to be constantly prepared for the challenges that come our way. However, learning isn't always going to be an easy process for some. In fact, for a lot of people, learning can be a very slow, gradual, and grueling experience with a lot of speed bumps, hurdles, and challenges. Not everyone is going to be equipped with faculties for learning, and that is why some people end up getting left behind.

Undoubtedly, the modern day we live in is a cutthroat world. In any industry, people are scrambling to make it to the top of their respective fields. There are various power vacuums that are just waiting to be filled left and right, and only those who have the know-how are going to be able to fill those positions.

It's all a matter of being able to equip oneself with the necessary tools that they might need to find success in life. That is exactly how learning plays a vital role in self-development and growth.

Charles Darwin explained it best in his Theory of Evolution. Only the strongest and fittest survive while the weak get left behind. This is a principle that has proven its authenticity time and time again throughout the history of human civilization. Those of us who are capable of adapting to our surroundings more quickly and effectively are the ones who are more likely to find success. Meanwhile, those who get a little too comfortable staying where they are will be the ones who will eventually falter. In spite of whatever circumstances one might have in life, people always have a choice whether or not to pursue opportunities for learning. Despite people's circumstances, people have the choice to seek out opportunities to learn. It's a level playing field for everyone, and it's all a matter of manifesting the will to act.

In the current state of our society, it's getting more and more difficult to stay ahead of the pack. Even though technology affords us with the tools that we might need to be armed with as we face everyday challenges, it can also serve as a major hindrance. You might think that technology is something that would enable learning and make it easier for people to acquire and develop new skills. However, there is a phenomenon called digital distraction. This is likely something that all of us are familiar with to a certain degree. In the advent of emerging technologies, it's not too farfetched to assume that people are prone to becoming more and more distracted. However, technology has evolved to a point where it has become a distraction. It used to be that people gradually adopted technology into their lives. But nowadays, human beings are born into technologically-dominated societies. They are essentially influenced by technology in their formative years, and it is now becoming a very integral aspect in the lives of many.

But how does digital distraction factor into one's capacity to learn?

Well, you need to be able to take a look at how human beings perceive survival and existence nowadays as opposed to how they used to in the early ages. Back in the infant stages of civilization, human beings were primarily concerned with the hunting and gathering of essentials like food, water, shelter, and clothing. Nothing else mattered much other than those basic necessities.

The world is no longer like that today. Society has evolved to become much more complex. The new age of civilization has brought about a species that still does prioritize the gathering of food, water, shelter, and clothing, but there is a whole new component that governs people's lives as well: information.

People are no longer just concerning themselves with the gathering of food anymore. People are prioritizing the gathering of information because they understand the importance of knowledge in this day and age. However, the acquisition of information has also been made a lot more complex due to the complications that are brought about by digital distractions. Even though technology primarily serves as a tool for human beings to be more productive and get work done more efficiently, it has also become one of the many potential distractions that keep us from focusing on what we need to be doing.

That is why in this age of information, it is very important that we can continually reassess the way that we approach learning and knowledge acquisition. It's not enough that we have the tools that we need to gather valuable information. It's essential that we are able to optimize the way that we process, retain, and apply everything we learn.

This eBook is going to be a contribution to that effort. There are indeed plenty of ways in which people can optimize the way they learn and sharpen the processes in which they acquire information. However, ironically enough, not a lot of people are going to be aware of these techniques. This is quite a shame especially in this day and age. A common concept that people have these days is that in the age of information, ignorance is a choice - and it's true. It's easy to pull up information with just a few taps and swipes of your fingertip. Yet, there are many people who choose to remain ignorant and unaware of the things that they could be up to speed on. In the modern era, you are going to need every competitive advantage that you can get. If you can further optimize how you acquire and process valuable information, then you are equipping yourself with skills that help improve you as a person.

Even though learning is truly a lifelong process, it shouldn't take you a lifetime to grasp and learn complex concepts. It would be an awful waste of time and energy if you devote your whole lifetime trying to master one particular discipline and disregard all the rest. It's like having the whole world out there available for you to see, and yet, you choose to lock yourself in your room your whole life. You shouldn't be afraid to pursue the study and mastery of different disciplines and topics. Time shouldn't be a hindrance or a limitation to your learning capacity. There are ways in which you can speed up the learning process so that you can make the most of your time. You can only dedicate so much time to learning after all. That is why you are going to want to capitalize on any methods that would help make that process easier and faster. Consider this your introduction to Accelerated Learning.

What is Accelerated Learning?

In a nutshell, Accelerated Learning (AL) is an emerging methodology that offers an innovative and comprehensive approach to increase one's capacity to absorb information, assess problems, and think of creative solutions. It is essentially a learning pedagogy that employs "brain-friendly" methods and techniques that further streamline and optimize the learning process as a whole. In order to gain a better understanding of what this theoretical framework is all about, it might be a good idea to first delve into its history and how this learning methodology came to be. From there, we can branch on to common techniques and tactics that fall under the Accelerated Learning pedagogy.

Accelerated Learning: A History

It all started with what was originally coined as Suggestopedia, a concept that was developed by respected Bulgarian professor and psychotherapist, Dr. Georgi Lozanov, back in the early 1970s. The famed professor founded the Suggestology Research Institute back in Bulgaria in 1966. It was through his work in the field wherein he was able to develop a groundbreaking teaching pedagogy that made the entire learning process easy and pleasurable. Various innovative tools were employed under his new framework in order to create a more interactive learning environment that included music, art, role-playing setups, and games. He was always someone who emphasized the importance of cultivating a learning environment that was optimized for the seamless transfer of knowledge. It was also of

Lozanov's opinion that it was the responsibility of the teacher to create a learning environment that is safe and stimulating and would inspire and motivate learners in order to maximize one's capacity to learn and absorb new ideas.

He stressed the point that the physical learning environment should always be one that invites learners to engage and interact with learning materials, facilitators, moderators, and fellow learners as well. It should be a learning space that not only takes into consideration a learner's mental state but emotional state as well, so as to offer a more holistic approach to tailored learning.

Dr. Lozanov truly advocated a renewed approach to learning and knowledge acquisition in order to keep modern society at the same pace as the rapid rate of technological advancement. He saw that society was evolving quickly and saw a need for the everyday human being to adapt in order for them to stay relevant and remain competitive. He also saw the potential risks involved with enforcing inefficient and ineffective learning pedagogies. He envisioned a learning methodology that would allow for a stress-free learning environment that would alleviate pressure brought about by contemporary learning institutions and education frameworks.

The term Suggestopedia is derived from the words "suggestion" and "pedagogy". It all centers around how a teacher or facilitator's words and actions might come across to the learner. Ultimately, the goal is for the teacher to suggest that learning and understanding a new idea is fun and easy. In addition, the idea of "suggestion" offers a sense of inclusivity on the part of the learner, allowing them to offer their insights on how they might be able to learn more efficiently and effectively.

It was 1976 in the United States when the name Suggestopedia was changed to Accelerated Learning. The name change was indicative of the cultural preferences of the time, and a desire to build upon adaptations that stemmed from Dr. Lozanov's original ideas that were developed over the years. At the same time, various leaps in the field of neuroscience and education psychology offered society a lot more insight into how to better approach the dynamics of teaching and learning. Numerous techniques and approaches to teaching and learning were curated over the years and were eventually collectively identified as methods of Accelerated Learning.

Accelerated Learning as We Know It Today

The Accelerated Learning philosophy can distinguish itself from other pedagogies purely from its foundations as a learning mechanism. It takes into consideration the suggestive factors that help influence a person's capacity to learn and absorb vital yet unfamiliar information. It is a pedagogy that heavily emphasizes the importance of the teacher and the facilitator in determining the ideal learning process of a student or learner.

Accelerated Learning can provide a real structure and system for teachers and facilitators to craft learning modules that would guarantee a learner's eventual success. It can also provide a learner an emphasis on student-centered learning. There is a lot of flexibility within the learning methodology itself to minimize the necessity for a student to make adjustments. The entire Accelerated Learning process has been further enriched and substantiated due to the scientific community's developed understanding of cognitive psychology, constructivism, multiple intelligences, neuro-linguistic programming, and more. There are all sorts of learning modules and activities that are implemented and experimented on throughout various class settings, and this is continually pushing the Accelerated Learning principles forward.

The whole idea behind Accelerated Learning is to offer every single individual an opportunity to learn any concept at their own preferred pace and with their preferred methodology. It is a learner-centric learning style that is more results-oriented than process-oriented. It does away with the whole notion of having one right way to go about learning a particular topic. Ultimately, it is a learning paradigm that is driven and motivated by the success of the learner.

How Do You Apply Accelerated Learning in Your Life?

If you happen to be someone who is as invested in learning as some people are, then this book is going to help you out in your endeavors. The very fact that you read books like this is evidence of your curiosity and your thirst for knowledge. We aren't always going to be given the set of tools that we want. That is why it's always best for us to make the most out of what we have. You can only do so much in this life if your capacity to learn is limited. You should always be making an effort to open your mind and free yourself from any intellectual or mental constraints that might be holding you back from acquiring new knowledge.

Studying more about accelerated learning techniques isn't just be designed to benefit you. If you are a manager, a CEO, a father, a mother, a teacher, a mentor, or whichever kind of influential figure that exists, you can greatly benefit from gaining a better understanding of how the human mind works and how you can most effectively initiate that transfer of knowledge from your brain into someone else's. Numerous organizations and big businesses all over the world are making use of accelerated learning techniques to train their employees to ensure seamless integration into the company's system. Transformative teachers in various academic fields make use of accelerated learning modules to further sharpen the intellect and knowledge of their students. There is a place for accelerated learning in anyone's life regardless if it's for personal use or to benefit someone else.

As human beings, we are all going to have our personal limitations. However, that shouldn't serve as a deterrent for our will and desire to pursue knowledge. So as long as you hold on to that desire, you are always going to have the potential to be an intellectual powerhouse. It all boils down to you being able to find the right approach to learning new things and acquiring new knowledge. That is exactly what this book is going to be able to provide you.

Some of the tips and techniques that will be listed in this book might be right up your alley and will be of great help to you, and some of it might not be. But that is the whole point of learning and education in the first place. It's about putting yourself out there with an open mind and a readied disposition towards learning. If one method works, then that's great. Stick with it. If it doesn't work, then learn from experience and continue pursuing new avenues for learning. Accelerated Learning isn't designed to be foolproof. It's still going to ultimately depend on the kind of personality that you have and your patience in finding what Accelerated Learning technique works best for you. Learning and self-education is a journey that only you can embark on by yourself. You can have mentors and resource materials, but the will to learn should still ultimately come from within. So, you've taken that first step. Now, it's time to move on to the next level.

Chapter 1: Learning as a Lifestyle

Before we move on to the techniques and methodologies that you can employ to gather and retain information more efficiently, it might be important to first make sure that you are in the right mental and physical capacity to do so. Sure, you can have your fill of all the best learning techniques and secrets in the world. But if you don't have a lifestyle and an attitude that primes you for learning, then you aren't really making the most out of the entire learning experience as a whole. That is why this chapter is going to focus on the various psychological and physiological facets of your learning process, and why it's just as important that you pay attention to these things as well.

It can be very difficult to make progress when you can't really visualize yourself going a certain distance in the first place. You always want to make sure that you believe in your capacity to absorb new information and develop new skills before you embark on your new journey of learning. It's okay that you might have a few hesitations and reservations because of some natural insecurities that you might have. However, it's always important that you believe that you have what it takes - mentally, emotionally, and physically - to accomplish your goals.

Priming the Mindset for Growth

Having a mindset that is primed and ready for growth and development is always going to be an important aspect of learning. In order for you to have that kind of mindset, you have to believe in your capacity to acquire skills, knowledge, and perspectives that you might not necessarily have yet. It's all about having faith in yourself and believing that you have what it takes to get to where you want to be. It's easier to focus on the task at hand when you aren't constantly being brought down by your fears and your insecurities, and so much simpler if all you have to worry about is developing a sense of mastery and competence over a certain discipline instead of worrying about how people might see you if you fail.

That doesn't mean that you look forward to receiving negative feedback from people who witness you on your journey. It just means that you are more open to this feedback because you understand that feedback is a tool that you can use and equip yourself with once you come face to face with new challenges and hurdles. You must always be able to make the transition from being someone who has a closed and fixed mindset to someone who has a more open and dynamic growth mindset. When you are more focused on the actual process of learning rather than just the results of it (whether positive or negative), it's a lot easier to keep on pushing forward regardless of the progress that you're making. How many times have you started a project only to find yourself quitting halfway because you aren't really feeling like you are making any progress? How many times have you talked yourself out of finishing a task just because you've felt like things haven't really gone the way you planned?

That's the problem with having a fixed mindset in learning. You tell yourself that you have to meet certain specifications and guidelines along the way to the point that you become inflexible and unadaptable. When your mindset is one that is primed for growth, you won't care about the stress of how much work you have left to do, you focus on being proud of how much you have already accomplished and how you still have so much more to gain from your hard work and persistence. As with any endeavor, persistence is always going to be key in learning. You may have already figured out that accelerated learning doesn't really promote a linear progression of growth and learning. It is more dynamic and sporadic than it is anything else. However, people with a healthy mindset for growth understand that little growth is better than no growth at all.

This is exactly the kind of philosophy that you need to adopt and set for yourself as you try to open yourself up to new ideas and lessons. Mastering any skill is never really designed to be easy after all. If it were, then everyone would be the master at everything. Yes, accelerated learning helps speed the process up and helps make your efforts a little more efficient and effective, but that doesn't mean that it's going to make everything easy. You are still going to have to face an uphill battle as you go along, and it's very important that you don't get intimidated by adversity whenever it strikes

Finding Motivation

Hard work equals success. That is probably something that you have always been taught since the moment you were born, and it's likely to be a piece of wisdom that you are going to pass on to others throughout your entire life. There is actually a lot of wisdom in this principle, but it doesn't always tell the whole story.

As a human being, you are entitled to have days where you feel like you just don't have the energy to keep going. Intrinsic motivation can be a very powerful thing to enable you to actually go out and pursue your goals and dreams. However, your energy will come and go. Intrinsic motivation isn't necessarily always going to be there for you, and it's true when they say that motivation on its own isn't really going to get you anywhere. It's more important that you are able to act on your motivation in order to manifest your dreams into reality. However, there is also no denying the fact that once a person is properly motivated, the entire process of learning will be a simpler and more enjoyable one. That is why you also need to be paying attention to what drives and motivates you as a learner.

First off, it might be important for you to understand what motivation really is and where it comes from. A lot of people have this false understanding of motivation and how it can be summoned at will. That isn't necessarily the case. You can't just tell yourself to "Get up and work!" all the time and actually expect it to work. Motivation is much like a plant in the sense that it needs to be cared for properly in order for it to bear fruit. Plenty of people are guilty of only fueling their motivations for long-term goals but not for short-term tasks. The problem with that is that it's the little day-to-day actions and bursts of effort that help us achieve our long-term goals.

For example, you might be motivated to get yourself promoted at work. This is something that you visualize for yourself every single day. Right when you wake up, you think about getting a promotion. When you fall asleep, you think about what your new office and higher salary is going to be like. This is good because you are motivating yourself for the long-term. However, you also need to cultivate the same kind of motivation for short-term goals. What do you need to do to get a promotion? You might need to increase sales and revenue, improve office efficiency, submit better-quality reports, or develop proficiency in a certain field that relates to your line of work. These are all the nitty-gritty aspects that go into achieving your long-term goal, but when you don't give yourself the motivation to do these things then it becomes harder to reach your overall goal. Sometimes, a little change in perspective can be enough. Try motivating yourself in a more concrete and more synthesized manner. It can go a long way in achieving your goals.

A Physiological Approach to Learning

It's not just the emotional or mental aspects of your character that you need to develop in order to maximize your capacity to learn, you must also pay attention to the physiological factors as well. Take a look at your working space or your office desk, how many distractions can you find there? Do you find yourself constantly browsing through your phone even though you should be focusing on an important document? Do you often try to watch an episode of Breaking Bad while trying to memorize legal jargon at the same time? Is there a crying baby right next to you while you're trying to familiarize yourself with the fundamentals of organizational management? Do you find yourself having to wipe off sweat every few minutes because of a lack of air conditioning in your room? These are all factors within your physical environment that impair your physiological ability to absorb new information. First of all, you always want to make sure that the environment in which you will be conducting your learning is a conducive one. You will find that having an environment that blocks out distractions is always going to be a better one to learn in.

In addition to that, you might also want to take note of the following tips:

- Engage in regular exercise. Studies have shown that engaging in regular exercise can improve a person's memory and thinking skills (Godman, 2014).

- Maintain a healthy and well-balanced diet. Research has proven that having poor nutritional habits can lead to compromised cognitive skills (Spencer, et al., 2017).

- Make sure that you get a good night's sleep. It's very important that you maintain a healthy sleep pattern as this can aid you in having good memory and ensuring that your brain is functioning at an optimal level (Potkin & Bunney, 2012).

Ultimately, you are the agent of learning here, and once the agent of learning is compromised, then the entire learning process as a whole is compromised. It doesn't matter what kind of revolutionary tactics or ground-breaking techniques you might be employing as you try to master a new skill or discipline, if you aren't in the right state to learn, then you aren't going to be performing at your full potential at all.

Chapter 2: DiSSS Method

Deconstruction - Selection - Sequencing - Stakes or the DiSSS method is a system of learning that was originally developed by Tim Ferriss, a successful author and television star. Ferriss has dedicated his life to the study of learning, and his findings eventually lead to the development of his DiSSS pedagogy.

Deconstruction

Try thinking of the most difficult item on your list of tasks at the moment. Could it be learning a new language? Could it be mastering the art of Olympic Weightlifting? Could it be learning how to do computer programming? These are all very admirable and respectable endeavors, but they are also very difficult skills to learn and master. You may hear someone speaking French fluently, and become intimidated by how difficult it all sounds. You may see a professional athlete lift a 200-pound barbell over their head, and you know that you would only end up in hospital if you tried doing it as well. You may have a friend who has made their own website from scratch while you struggle with customizing your own Facebook page. It's always intimidating whenever take on a new goal and look at it in its totality. That is why the idea of Conceptual Deconstruction or more plainly, "deconstruction", is a very effective way to go about learning and achieving something.

Any skill that you might look to acquire in life or any discipline that you seek to master is going to have parts, it's going to have layers. The person who you see speaking French fluently didn't learn to do so in a day. There are facets of the French language that can be broken down and deconstructed into various parts such as vocabulary, grammar, diction, and more. All those major concepts can be broken down even further. Once you just slowly break it down little by little, you will discover that the feat of learning a new language isn't going to be as impossible as you might have initially thought. When you are done with deconstructing the aspects of your learning process, then you can proceed to the second phase of learning: Selection.

Selection

When you enroll in a class, it's likely that the teacher is going to outline this really long syllabus for you that you are going to have to follow in a linear fashion in order for you to complete the course. And even then, it's not an assurance that you will have mastered the skill by the end of it. However, with the DiSSS method, you don't always have to be learning a new skill in a linear fashion, especially if that's a method that doesn't really work well for you. You've already completed the deconstruction phase of the learning process, and now it is time for you to move on to the Selection phase of it.

The Selection phase of the DiSSS accelerated learning method is designed for you to be efficient with the time and energy that you put into mastering a new skill. You might not always be afforded with the luxury of having lots of time that you would be able to dedicate to learning a new craft. That is why it's always important that you stay organized with the way that you distribute your time. This is where the Selection phase comes in. You are going to have to really take a look at your goals and what you hope to achieve and learn to prioritize based on your analysis of the situation. It's important that you first dedicate most of your time and your energy to the aspects of the skill that would help you reach your desired level of competency the quickest.

To further illustrate this point, let us go back to the example of mastering the French language. For most people, it would take an average of around 6-12 months to become fluent in any language. However, with the DiSSS method, it's very much possible for you to know everything that you need to know about a new language in around 8-12 weeks. How? Why is there such a drastic disparity? Well, it's all about selection. You won't know *as much* as you would if you took 6-12 months to study the language, but if you learn to dedicate your time appropriately, you are going to know everything that you need to know in just 8-12 weeks. The principle of selection is more concerned with what you're studying than it is with how you are studying it.

If you enroll in a typical French language class, you might be taught the French equivalent of words like church, father, school, office, house, run, jump, walk, etc. Some of these words might be useful to your everyday life, but some of them might not be. The whole point of selection is for you to choose roughly around 1,500-2,000 words that you would commonly use on a daily basis and focus on mastering those words. There's no point in mastering the entirety of the French dictionary if you aren't going to be using a majority of those words anyway. It would merely be a lot of wasted time and effort.

By focusing on specific aspects of the skill that you're looking to master, it would be a more practical and pragmatic approach to learning. It would offer you a more efficient use of the time and energy that you dedicate to the mastery of this new skill. Learning is always most effective when importance and value is attributed to the ideas that are being absorbed by the agent. A person is much more inclined to learn something that they can apply to their daily life than something that only exists in theory.

Sequencing

Once the selection phase in the learning process has been completed, the sequencing phase follows. This exposes the ineffectiveness of a prescribed linear method of learning. It's not just about figuring out the important aspects of a topic or discipline that you need to be learning. It's also about figuring out what you should be addressing right away when you begin the learning process. This is exactly where proper sequencing should come in.

Tim Ferriss explained the importance of being able to sequence tasks in an efficient and effective manner. In *The Tim Ferriss Experiment*, he takes on all kinds of challenges that revolve around him trying to learn new skills within a short period of time. He has successfully taken on various tasks including learning how to drive race cars, learning a new language, and mastering chess. The whole DiSSS method is his brainchild and this is how he describes the "Sequencing" phase of the learning technique.

Ferris claims that putting various phases and steps in the right order is crucial in efficient and effective learning. He says that you don't always have to start at the "start" in order to master a new skill. For instance, when he was learning how to master chess from an expert, they didn't begin the lesson with the starting moves that one would employ in a typical game. Instead, they jumped right into some very specific moves that people tend to encounter a lot in the middle of chess games. With proper sequencing, you don't always have to start at the beginning in order to start things off the right way.

Stakes

The last phase of the DiSSS Method is Stakes. Sometimes, in order to add a little more motivation for a person to learn something new within a short period of time, there have to be certain stakes involved. Your partner isn't going to break up with you if you can't learn to speak French. You aren't going to lose your job if you are incapable of defeating a chess master. That's why it's so easy for you to just abandon a task altogether with the mindset that you can always pick things up later on. You don't really have an incentive to put in the time and effort that you need to master a particular skill.

That's why it might be a good idea for you to incentivize yourself. Ferriss suggests what is most often referred to as a "commitment device." A good example of this would be you giving your partner control of your credit card for a full shopping spree in case you fail to meet your goal within a specified amount of time. You want to be able to feel the disappointment of you failing to meet a certain goal, and sometimes, losing money can be a good incentive for you to try harder. It's really as simple as that. You want to add a little pressure and heat to your learning experience so that you don't get tempted to slack off.

Chapter 3: Mixing Things Up with Interleaved Practice

Focused learning efforts are always great for a lot of people who want to see immediate results and feel instant gratification. Even though this might seem like focused studying is a great way to go about accelerating the learning process, it turns out that it might not necessarily be the case. For most skills, disciplines, and trades, it's rarely ever going to be a one-dimensional case. There are always going to be further layers to mastering a new art form or discipline. For example, learning geometry isn't just about memorizing names of shapes and figures. It is also a matter of learning formulas and mathematical applications. When you are learning about the stock market, you have to familiarize yourself with companies' stock profiles and histories. You also have to be familiar with stock market theory and application. You must also learn about projections, financial literacy, market trends, and other technicalities. Mastery is never going to be a one-dimensional affair. There are various skills and facets to mastering a discipline that needs to be taken into consideration. Even though it can be tempting to take it one facet at a time, there is research that suggests that it would be more effective to juggle learning multiple skills at once.

Intuitively, you might think that focusing all of your energy and attention on a single skill or discipline is going to be the most efficient and effective way to develop proficiency and mastery. When you are in school, there is a specific period dedicated to Math, Science, Art, Music, English, Physical Education, and so on. For each specific subject or discipline, they are going to focus on just one particular concept within a specified amount of time. Once that time is up, students move on to another class where they will have to focus all of their attention on another individual concept and topic.

This kind of learning is often referred to as the "block method" of learning. It might make sense to a lot of people considering that it is standard practice in traditional educational archetypes. However, there is reason to believe that figuring how to appropriately space out one's learning sessions by diversifying the learning materials and topics for every session might prove to be a more effective method of learning as a whole. This is often what is referred to as "spaced learning," and is gaining vast popularity in various education circles.

Spaced learning is essentially the consistent return to a particular topic at set intervals over the span of a few weeks (or months, depending on the depth of what you are studying). It works in contrast with merely studying one particular topic over an extended period of time before moving on to another topic. This method of distributing learning sessions and mastery might seem very complex and hectic considering that you will have to be juggling so many things at once. But there is a way to make this method more efficient and effective than traditional methods of learning and study.

The process of being able to efficiently space your learning out is called interleaved practice, and that is precisely the learning pedagogy that will serve as the central topic and theme of this chapter. When you can efficiently interleave various disciplines and practices into a single study session, you are covering a lot more ground within a short amount of time.

According to Benedict Carey, bestselling author of *How We Learn: The Surprising Truth About When, Where, and Why It Happens*, the smarter approach to accelerated learning would be to take on multiple facets of a specific discipline at once (Carey, 2014). When you focus on one particular aspect of learning, it can be easy to track your progress within a short amount of time. For example, if you're learning how to play guitar, it can be very easy to feel like you are making a lot of progress when you are only focused on memorizing the chords. However, with this method of learning, you are also neglecting other essential aspects of learning how to play guitar such as scales, strumming patterns, keys, and more. You might be mastering one aspect of playing guitar, but you are far from mastering the musical instrument as a whole. Carey suggests that it would be much better to juggle learning various skills within a single practice or learning session instead. Even though progress might seem slower in the short-term, it offers a more holistic approach to learning which would pay off in the long-term. A more holistic understanding of a particular theory or discipline would always be a much more efficient approach to learning than focusing your efforts on one facet at a time.

Another great example would be the art of mastering mixed martial arts or MMA. This form of fighting or athletic training incorporates various forms of martial arts and physical conditioning. You are going to want to develop basic skills in striking and grappling, while also making sure that you have the strength, stamina, coordination, speed, and endurance that you might need to succeed in the sport. During your training or practice sessions, instead of focusing on just one aspect of MMA per session, it might be a good idea to touch on various aspects of it. You might feel like you are making substantial progress within a single session if you just dedicate the entire practice session to your striking skills, or you might feel dramatic improvements after just a couple of sessions of practicing your striking techniques. However, you aren't taking into consideration the fact that you are neglecting all the other aspects of mixed martial arts that are integral to your success. Based on Carey's theory, it would be much better to integrate striking, cardiovascular training, strength training, and grappling into a single session. You might not see instant improvement in any of these facets, and progress might feel slow, but ultimately, you are making much more progress towards the bigger goal. This method of practicing and learning is more about making progress in the grander scheme of things within a short period of time.

This learning method also enforces the idea of the human agent being capable of juggling various skills and disciplines at any given moment. The human capacity to learn works at its best whenever it is constantly being tested and pushed to its limits. But again, how do you know when you're doing interleaved practice correctly? How do you figure out if you're being inefficient with your practice or not? These are perfectly valid questions to ask. There is indeed a proper and efficient way to go about interleaved practice. You are just going to want to make sure that you remember these 4 main principles:

Ensure that the skills and disciplines you interleave are related

At first glance, interleaved practice is only going to seem chaotic because the idea of incorporating different topics or disciplines into a single study session sound completely overwhelming. However, the true purpose of interleaved practice isn't for you to cram random topics and ideas into a single session of learning and practicing. You always have to make sure that your interleaved skills and disciplines are related to one another. For example, you aren't going to want to merge studying music theory and practicing basketball into a single practice session. That just wouldn't make sense. However, it would be a lot easier to manage that "chaos" if you incorporate harmony, music history, musical scaling, and rhythm into a single practice session. All of these topics and ideas are interrelated, and there is a way to connect all of them underneath one big umbrella of learning.

Interleaved practice can only seem messy and disorganized when you're not going about it in the right way. However, if you find a way to relate all of the interleaved disciplines that you are incorporating into your practice, then everything is going to start to make better sense. It is like playing multiple notes in unison to produce a beautiful harmony.

Study in a non-linear fashion

Spontaneity, dynamism, and organized randomness - this is the very essence of interleaved practice. You are going to want to do away with a linear style of learning. You don't have to always start at point A before you can get to point B. You don't always have to complete every task at point C before you can start your journey towards point D. With interleaved practice, you are juggling multiple skills and disciplines at once. You are on your way to point B even though you aren't necessarily done with point A. You are already making progress towards point D even though you haven't touched on point C just yet. Interleaved practice frees up your learning schedule by allowing you to work on different things at once.

However, there is still some sense of order and organization behind all of this supposed chaos. You want to make sure that you are still actively tracking all of the progress that you are making in various fields. Ideally, you will want to be holistic in your approach to self-development. That means that while it would be ideal for you to excel in one or two different fields, you never want to compromise or neglect the other disciplines in your practice. It's all about balance. Yes, you might be more proficient at one aspect of your practice over the others, but as much as possible, you are going to want to make sure that you develop a sense of mastery and proficiency in all aspects of your practice.

Incorporate other learning strategies into your interleaved practice

Don't be afraid of incorporating a lot of the other accelerated learning methodologies that you will read in this book into your interleaved practice. For instance, you might want to make use of binaural beats for focus as you engage in your interleaved practice study sessions. You might not know what binaural beats are just yet, but you will, so long as you continue reading this book. Transformative learning means being able to do away with traditional methods of learning to make way for revolutionary learning tactics. You should never be afraid of getting creative and incorporating practices that would better serve your personal study habits.

Interleaved practice merely serves as a general guiding principle which you can follow throughout your learning process. That doesn't mean that it's a completely inflexible practice that won't allow for the incorporation of other learning techniques and methodologies. You might want to make use of flashcards or mnemonic devices. These are also accelerated learning methodologies that you are going to eventually read about as you make your way through this book. Ultimately, there are limitless possibilities for changes and additions you can make to the interleaved practice philosophy of learning. You just have to get creative. Think outside of the box.

Don't quit at the lack of instant gratification

One of the most discouraging aspects of interleaved practice is that it doesn't produce dramatic results right away. It can be very disheartening for the learner to feel like not much progress has been made in spite of juggling multiple topics and ideas within a single learning session each time. It's practically information overload during every practice, and the amount of effort and focus required to be fully engaged the whole time can be very overwhelming. It would be easier to bear the workload if the results are seen, felt, or experienced. However, results aren't always going to come right away. That's why it can be incredibly tempting to quit right at the start.

But that is the kind of mindset you have to do away with if you're engaged in interleaved practice. The results that you seek aren't going to be immediate. However, you have to remind yourself that you aren't playing the short game here. You are studying for the long haul. You just have to be able to trust in the process and believe that every single effort that you put into your practice today is going to pay off in the long run.

Chapter 4: PACER Method

Joe McCullough, author of *Accelerated Learning for Students: Learn More in Less Time*, is an Accelerated Learning aficionado whose works have been used and followed by learners and knowledge seekers all over the world. Aside from being a published author, he also runs a blog that is dedicated to learning techniques and methodologies. In one of his more popular posts, he highlights the PACER method which he developed himself. He claims that the PACER method is one that can be followed by anyone to suit any pursuit for learning and mastery (McCullough, 2013). The method is actually broken down into 5 different steps, which make up the PACER acronym. Here are all the specific steps to the PACER method:

Prepare Your State of Learning

According to McCullough, the very first thing that you have to do when you begin learning a new skill or mastering a new art form, it's very important that you first prepare your mentally, emotionally, and physically. You must always make it a point to place yourself in a positive headspace. You need to be motivating yourself intrinsically, and it can be very hard to tap into that motivation when there are just too many negative blockages that are preventing you from doing so. It is absolutely essential that you are fully engaged, locked in, and focused on everything that you're going to have to do. As they say sometimes, the hardest part is finding the motivation to start. But what they don't tell you is that you also have to start things off the right way.

If you embark on a new learning project on a negative note, then you are essentially just setting yourself up for failure. You don't want to be shooting yourself in the foot right out the gate, do you? One huge aspect of finding success in learning is in cultivating an environment that sets you up for success, but not a lot of people realize that it's just as important to establish an internal state of mind and being that optimizes the entire learning process as a whole. You want to make sure that you have a headspace that is confident, positive, resourceful, and open before you embark on your learning journey.

Acquire the Skills and Knowledge

Once you are in an optimal state to learn, you must now acquire the necessary skills and knowledge to master whatever discipline you are interested in. That all starts with you first coming to terms with what the big picture is. You must first be able to understand the entire subject just so that you can gain a holistic and well-rounded understanding of what it is you are getting yourself into. Once you get a good grasp of the overview of a subject matter, you are essentially giving your brain a glimpse of the entire journey that it's about to embark upon. You might not have all of the specifics just yet, but you know where to start, where you need to go, and what you need to do in order to get there. Once you are able to understand and grasp all of these things, then you would be better able to determine the best approach for you to achieve your goals. Now, you will be able to determine which learning and communication style would suit you best for the task at hand.

Findings in the field of Neurolinguistic Programming, or NLP, have identified three particular learning styles: visual, auditory, and kinesthetic. It's important to note that everyone is capable of learning and absorbing information using all three styles. However, some people are better at processing new information and unfamiliar concepts with one or two particular styles. If you understand what your preferred learning style is, you are going to want to bank on that and really adopt that method when it comes to learning. This is when you start to really absorb all of the nitty gritty details that you need to gain competency and mastery in the discipline that you are refining.

Cement your Learning

Once you have successfully absorbed all of this new information, it is absolutely essential that you are able to cement all of this data into your long-term memory. There's no point in taking the time and using up your energy to learn all of these new concepts only for you to forget about them later on. It would end up being a total waste of time and effort on your part if you fail to permanently ingrain these lessons into your mind. That is why the third phase of the PACER method is for you to cement your learning. You want to make sure that the lessons that you are absorbing are stored in your mind's internal hard drive.

You can best retain your memory of these lessons and concepts by putting them to use in a practical capacity. According to McCullough, there is research out there that supports the idea of people being able to remember concepts better if they are able to apply them to everyday life. For instance, if you have taken it upon yourself to learn more about interior design, then perhaps you can take all of the theoretical concepts that you are learning about and apply it to your daily life. Take some time to apply design changes in your work or living spaces. If you are learning about music theory and you are currently studying the topic of scales, then grab a musical instrument and start practicing those scales. Being able to put these concepts to practical use is going to help you memorize them for the long term.

Examine and Embrace

This phase of the PACER method might be taking a page out of the traditional style of formal education, but it's important that you are able to test yourself and gauge your progress so far. This means that aside from just putting what you've learned to use, you are going to want to measure just how far you have come in terms of your learning process. The goal of this particular phase is for you to force yourself to remember and recap everything that you have picked up so far. In addition to that, you are also going to want to see if you've missed out on anything or if there are any gaps in your knowledge. You want to make sure that you have established a structure and foundation for your learning, but you also want to make sure that there aren't any cracks that you may have left unchecked.

Once you feel like you are content with what you have learned so far, now is the time for you to apply everything and make use of it. If you have been learning how to play the piano, perhaps you can try auditioning for a band or putting on a private show for your friends. If you have been mastering the art of architecture, maybe you can try applying for a job or internship at an architecture firm. Embrace all of the knowledge that you've acquired and apply them to your life in a meaningful way.

Review, Revise, and Reward

This is now the final step of the PACER method: Review, Revise, and Reward. You have to go over the entire learning process as a whole and analyze just how well (or how badly) it might have worked for you. When you engage in these methods of self-assessment and reflection, you are also developing your understanding of learning, growth, and development. As you might have already figured out by now, learning isn't necessarily going to be a linear process. It's going to require a lot of analysis, revision, and regrouping as well. You aren't constantly moving forward. That's why it's important that you are able to look back and spot any potential areas for improvement as you pursue learning in the future.

Additionally, you want to be able to celebrate and reward yourself to a certain degree. You set out a goal for yourself and you delivered. You committed yourself to a particular task, and you saw it through all the way to the end. This is something that you should definitely be proud of, and you shouldn't be afraid of celebrating it.

Chapter 5: Mind Mapping

The process of mind mapping isn't necessarily a new one. It is a very effective tool in organizing one's thoughts so as to create a clean, orderly, and structured path towards learning. The human mind has a tendency to be very cluttered, sporadic, and just plain chaotic a lot of the time. This can make the learning process very difficult as the brain can only devote so much of its power to specific ideas and concepts.

In a popular TEDx Talk conducted by Hazel Wagner, Ph.D. in November of 2017, she made a case for mind mapping as being a very effective tool for accelerated learning. The full TEDxNaperville talk is available to view on YouTube and has garnered nearly 900,000 views as of this writing. Wagner has been a learner her whole life and has more than 4 degrees, including a Ph.D. in Mathematics. In the video, she claims that mind mapping has aided her in tasks that require understanding, memorization, and retention. She specializes in the theory of mind mapping, and has committed herself to teaching others about how it can aid in memory enhancement, planning, studying, and more.

She says that mind mapping is a method in which a person takes notes while strengthening their memory. The entire method is designed in a way that encourages healthy brain function and cognitive performance instead of holding it back. She claims that the standard method of notetaking is counterproductive to learning because it is essentially the equivalent of transcribing. Taking notes is never an effective method of learning because it takes away the analysis, understanding, and eventual absorption of a topic. The mental faculties required to engage in note-taking would take away from one's ability to analyze and learn more effectively.

Mind mapping, Wagner says, is a more mentally participative form of note-taking because it recruits various parts of the brain that require analysis, absorption, and retention. Wagner claims that the brain doesn't store entire paragraphs or sentences, and so it would be pointless to take down notes of entire paragraphs and sentences. Instead, she postulates that the brain stores ideas, images, and connections between principles, concepts, and lessons.

It's not just Wagner who is serving as a major proponent for mind mapping as an effective tool for learning and knowledge acquisition. Advocates of mind mapping say that when you engage in the process of breaking down big ideas into simpler, smaller concepts for you to study and analyze, it becomes easier for the brain to understand and retain all of that information. To fully maximize the effects of mind mapping for accelerated learning, you might want to consider following these steps (depending on what you're studying and what your goals are, you might be able to skip one or more of these steps):

Focus on the Main Central Theme

First of all, you are going to want to begin your mind map with the central theme of what you want to study. Your mind map can't be composed of different concepts and topics right off the bat. Every single idea that you are going to study and master has to stem from one overarching idea, and that is what should serve as the central theme of your mind map. Everything has to be able to connect to what your central theme is going to be. It's the foundation of your house. It's the trunk of your tree. It's the blank canvas on which you are going to be painting your mind map masterpiece.

Once you are able to establish what the central theme of your mind map is going to be, move on to secondary themes. Make sure that all of your secondary themes have direct links to the central themes. Once you feel like you have completed the secondary themes, move on to the tertiary themes, and so on. Continue this process until you feel like you have covered all the bases. Make sure that all connections and links are in the right place before you move on to the next phase of mind mapping.

Synthesize All of the Data

Your mind map might still be a little clunky and messy at this point, but that's okay. That is something that is to be expected and is perfectly normal. It's during this step wherein all the cleaning up of that data is going to take place. Take a long hard look at your mind map, and try to assess which ideas are important and which ones aren't. Try touching on every single idea, and if it feels like it's leading you away from the central theme of the mind map, then just abandon it entirely and move on to another. If you feel like one particular idea is helping you get to your goals, then try to extract as much as you can out of it. Do your research, and read up on anything and everything that you deem to be important. This is where you weed out everything that might not have value and hone in on the things that do.

Make Use of Visual Aids and Imagery

To help retain of all this data, try to make use of visual aids and imagery. It's not enough that you fill your mind map up with a bunch of words and long paragraphs. In order to drive the point home even more, you are going to want to incorporate visual aids or other forms of sensory clues that can help you identify a concept or an idea better.

Create Visual Presentations

Once you feel like you already have a rough draft of your mind map, then it might be best for you to formalize everything that you have learned into an organized visual presentation that you could show to peers and colleagues. There are two reasons for this particular step: for one, it would force you to really see just how much information you have acquired over the course of your studies. And secondly, your ability to communicate these ideas and lessons to other people in visual form would gauge just how well you understand a particular topic or discipline. When you create your visual presentation, remember to keep the following things in mind:

- Summarize the entire learning process

- Always base your learnings on accurate information

- Develop your own thoughts and ideas on the learning materials that you made use of

Gather Feedback from Others

Lastly, you might want to consider gathering feedback from other people. One key aspect of learning anything in life is knowing that you aren't always going to be able to see things from every perspective. You aren't always going to have the answer. That is why there is always going to be inherent value in seeking out the perspective and thoughts of other people. Don't be afraid of presenting your mind map to someone who you might consider to be your senior or mentor in the field. Once you are open-minded and humble enough to be able to take in external feedback, you are further improving your capacity to learn and absorb new information that might be of value to you in the future.

Chapter 6: Mnemonic Devices

There are certain things that are just easier to recall from the back of your mind than others. For example, it's easy to remember a negative remark that was made several weeks ago by a work superior about your performance at the office. But at the same time, you're going to struggle with keeping track of all the important details that were discussed in your office meeting this morning. Why is that the case? Why is one memory so vivid while the other? This is not really a rare occurrence in people. In fact, it happens often and there's a reason for it. The ironic truth of it all is that it is much more challenging to remember the things that you *want* to remember over random memories in your brain that you just can't seem to get rid of. You've probably been stumped in the middle of a meeting trying to recall a valuable piece of information that would help your presentation. But then, you have no problem reciting lines of a poem that you read back when you were in elementary school. This is all happening by design, and there is no randomness about it at all. There is a very specific reason why you are able to remember certain things and why you forget others.

This is precisely where mnemonics come in, and this chapter is going to devote itself to the art of using mnemonic devices to help improve memory and knowledge retention. In a nutshell, a mnemonic device is essentially any word, image, phrase, or sound that you might be able to attribute to a particular idea. The whole mnemonic system is built on the principle of you attributing a complex and hard-to-remember detail to something to a familiar concept that is easier for you to grasp. One very popular mnemonic device that is widely used today is designed to teach kids the proper order of the planets in the Solar System:

My Very Excellent Mother Just Served Us Nine Pizzas

If you take the first letter of every word in that very distinct and easy-to-remember sentence, then you would be able to easily remember the proper order of the planets in the Solar System:

Mercury, Venus, Earth, Mars, Jupiter, Saturn, Uranus, Neptune, and Pluto

Okay, they say that Pluto isn't really a planet anymore, but you get the point of the mnemonic device. This mnemonic phrase is considered to be an Acrostic Mnemonic one wherein the first letters of the words are used to represent the clues for what you are trying to remember. Not all mnemonic devices are designed to be this way though. For instance, when teaching toddlers how to write for the first time, this mnemonic device is often used to differentiate lower case "b" and "d" while writing:

"B" stands for bright so put the circle on the right.

This mnemonic device, in particular, incorporates the use of rhyme and visual imagery to help drive the point home. There are also other visual images that people can draw up in their minds which can be used as mnemonic devices. For example, when trying to remember how to properly spell the word "necessary," one merely has to recall the image of a shirt. On a regular shirt, there is only one collar and two sleeves. In the word "necessary," there is only one "C" and two "S" letters.

Mnemonic devices can come in handy whenever you are trying to learn very technical terms which you might not use on a daily basis just yet. It also helps if you are able to make a connection between the mnemonic device and the piece of information that you are trying to recall in your mind. A good example would be if you were studying religion and you had to remember the first five books of the Old Testament. The mnemonic device highlighted in this example is going to harbor a connection between itself and the themes of the topic that you are trying to learn:

God Equals Light Not Darkness could help you remember that the first five books of the Old Testament are Genesis, Exodus, Leviticus, Numbers, and Deuteronomy.

One of the great things about mnemonic devices is that you don't necessarily have to get creative with them if you don't want to. If you are studying a relatively common or popular academic field, then there is likely a mnemonic device out there that can help you with your studies. Even a simple internet search would be enough to help you find some great mnemonic devices that you can incorporate into your own study routine. However, mnemonics are always most effective whenever you take the time to construct them on your own. Even though this might not be a technique that comes naturally to you at first, it's something that you are going to eventually be able to get used to.

If you are more musically-inclined than most people, it might also be a good idea to use songs or music as a mnemonic device. It might be easier to attribute or associate certain complex terms and ideas with songs that are already familiar to you. Maybe studying a complex topic with a particular song playing in the background can help you remember these ideas better by merely recalling the song that you've associated them with. For instance, replacing key words in a song's lyrical structure that you know by heart can aid in memorization.

Chapter 7: The Art of Speed Reading

Books are always going to play a constant role in media and academics. In spite of the technological revolution that has ushered in the use of computers, tablets, and phones, books still hold their place as an important source of information. Sure, you can always do a quick Google search when you want to find out more about a certain topic. You might watch a short YouTube video to in order to summarize the things that took place during The French Revolution or The Cold War. However, people are always going to naturally gravitate towards reading books in order to learn as much as they can about a specific topic that piques their interest.

However, the problem with books is that they can be really hard to read through in a single sitting. Have you ever found yourself opening a book and reading the same sentence over and over again for five minutes straight? Not a very efficient way to go about studying, is it? Well, this is a common problem that a lot of people face, and you shouldn't feel bad about it. This chapter is going to help you and everyone who has a problem with reading more effectively. As you make your way through this chapter, you will learn how to speed up the time it might take you to read a book, and it will also help you with common retention techniques that you can use to remember what you read.

There is a case to be made for speed reading as being the most important skill for you to learn and develop if you really want to make the most out of your potential to learn. The higher the speed in which you are able to absorb information, then the more efficient you will be with the time and effort that you put into learning. According to a report on speed reading by Forbes magazine, studies show that the average adult reads around 300 words per minute (Nelson, 2012). At that rate, it would take people roughly around 3-4 hours to read an average-length nonfiction book. If you are looking to read one or two books a week, this might prove to be problematic seeing as it is very hard for a working adult in the modern world to find that much extra time in a day to devote to reading. This is exactly where the art of speed reading comes in.

Referencing more work from Tim Ferriss and his research on learning and productivity, he states that the speed reading technique can increase a person's reading speed by as much as 300% (2009). He outlines his speed reading technique in a module called The PX Project, which can be completed in a span of 3 hours and is designed to dramatically increase a person's reading speed. Highlighted in this chapter are the various phases of the PX Project and the steps you need to take to improve your personal reading speed.

Preparation

The first thing that you are going to need in order to carry this project out is a book that you have never read before. Ideally it would be a nonfiction book, and it would have at least 200 pages. You should also have some kind of stopwatch or countdown timer ready with you as well.

Definitions and Distinctions of the Reading Process

Now that you have the physical tools that you need to conduct the project, it is now important that you first familiarize yourself with the basic definitions and distinctions that actually make up the reading process.

Minimize the Duration and Number of Fixations Per Line

Contrary to popular belief, you do not necessarily need to read a sentence in a single linear fashion taking it one word at a time. You can actually read in a jumping fashion, bouncing from one segment of a line to another. These are called saccades or saccadic movements. After every saccade that you perform, you temporarily pause and take a mental snapshot of where your eyes are fixated upon. Each standard fixation is going to last for around 0.25-0.5 seconds. In order to read faster, you are going to want to minimize the duration and the number of fixations that you have per line.

Eliminate Regression and Back-Skipping

For untrained readers, regression and back-skipping are consistent bad habits that occur while reading. Regression is the act of consciously rereading a single line or phrase over and over again. Back-skipping is the wrongful fixation of previously covered spots on the page. Not a lot of people realize that this can really add on to a person's reading time. In fact, it can even take up as much as 30% of a person's total reading duration.

Increase Horizontal Peripheral Vision and Number of Words Registered Per Fixation

For the untrained reader, it is common to employ a central focus without making use of horizontal peripheral vision while reading. This can leave out up to 50% of words within a single fixation.

Protocol

With the protocol, you are going to be briefed on the proper technique in reading, the proper applications of these techniques through conditioning, and the proper testing methods to gauge your reading efficiency and comprehension.

These goals and facets to the protocol are all separate and you need to focus on them all on an individual basis. If you are working on the speed of your reading, then you shouldn't be worrying about comprehension. In order to yield the best possible results, you are going to want to practice reading at around 3x the speed of your target reading speed. For example, you might currently be reading at 300 wpm and you hope to get your speed up to 800 wpm. Then that means that you will have to practice reading at a rate of 2400 wpm. There will be two main techniques that will be discussed in this introduction:

- Trackers and pacers, to address prolonged fixation, regression, and back-skipping.

- Perceptual expansion, to address central focus fixation.

Determine a Baseline

In order for you to determine your current reading speed, take the book that you have prepared prior to the start of this project and count the total number of words in 5 lines and then divide it by 5. The quotient should be the average number of words per line.

So, if you have 65 words after 5 lines of writing, then you would have to divide 65 by 5. The answer you would get is 13. Therefore, you have an average of 13 words per line. After that, count the total number of lines on 5 pages, and then divide the total number by 5 in order to get your average number of lines per page. If there are 155 lines after 5 pages, then your average number of lines per page would be 31. After that, multiply the average number of words per line and the average number of lines per page.

In this case, you would have to multiply 13 and 31. The answer you would get is 403. That would be the average words per page.

Once you are finished with all the calculations, you can then start to test your reading speed. Set your countdown timer for 1 minute and proceed to read as you would normally. Don't speed through your reading. Read with proper comprehension. After one minute, multiply the number of total lines you have read by the average words per line in order for you to determine your baseline reading rate of words per minute.

Trackers and Pacers

As mentioned, the trackers and pacers are used to address the issues that you have with prolonged fixations, regressions, and back-skipping. The importance of the tracker is going to be emphasized as you are going to delve deeper into what you can do to really improve your reading speed. Think back to when you were counting the number of words and lines in your book. Did you make use of some kind of pointer like a finger or a pen?

If you did, then that's essentially the explanation of why a tracker is important. You need a visual aid to help determine the accuracy and efficiency of your fixation patterns. In order for you to condition yourself to read faster, it's important that you are able to get rid of things that are making your reading process inefficient as a whole.

For the purposes of this exercise, you should make use of a pen. Draw an invisible underline as you read through each line while maintaining the point of your fixation right on top of the pen. This dynamic point serves as your tracker and pacer to help you maintain a consistent speed as you are reading.

First, you will want to work on technique. For the tracking phase, you must get rid of your need to comprehend what you are reading. What is important is that your fixation is able to seamlessly move through the line in no more than one second.

Use the pen as your tracker and your pacer as you read through every line. Again, make sure that each line doesn't take more than one second to read. Do this for about 2 minutes straight.

Next, you are going to want to up the tempo a little bit. Perform the same tracking task as previously explained without paying any attention to comprehension. Focus entirely on speed. Except now, you have to read the entire line in less than half a second. That's right. Half a second. And you're going to want to do so for the entirety of 3 minutes. Really focus on the exercise at hand and don't let up until the alarm sounds.

Perceptual Expansion

Now, it is time for you to work on your perceptual expansion. Try looking at the middle of your computer screen or phone screen. Focus at the exact center of the screen. If you are focusing on the right area, you would still be able to perceive and register the sides of the screen. This is called your peripheral vision, and a lot of the time, your peripheral vision is disregarded when reading. If you really want to increase your reading speed, you are going to have to maximize your peripheral vision in your reading technique as well.

Again, in order for you to train this skill properly, you might want to recruit the services of a pen as a tracker.

For the technique phase of this skill, you are going to want to use as a pen to pace your reading at no slower than one line per second. Begin reading one word in from the first word of every line, and end one word out from the last word of every line. Again, in this phase, you will want to forgo comprehension. That is not the point of the exercise at the moment. Make sure that you don't exceed the duration of one second for every line. Do this for one minute straight.

For the second portion of the technique phase, do the same as the previous portion, except increase the number of words. So, instead of starting with one word in and ending with one word out, you will want to do so with two words. However, it's important that you still maintain a reading speed of no more than one line per second. Do this for one minute straight.

For the speed phase of this skill, you will now want to start 3 words in for every line and end 3 words out every line. Repeat the same technique without exceeding more than 0.5 seconds for every line. Do this for 3 minutes straight.

It's likely that you aren't going to comprehend anything throughout this entire phase of the practice. However, that really isn't the point of this exercise just yet. You are merely working on your technique and your speed. Comprehension will come once you are able to gain proficiency in your technique. Just make sure that you always stay focused on what you are reading and do not allow your mind to wander.

Calculate Your New Reading Speed (WPM)

Now, it's time to calculate your new reading speed and see how you've progressed so far. As you did at the beginning of this exercise, set your timer for one minute and begin reading at your fastest comprehension rate. At the end of the minute, multiply the number of lines that you read by what you previously determined to be your average words per line. The product of this is going to be your new reading speed or words per minute rate.

Application

If you have been disciplined and committed in your practice in speed reading, then you will have developed a proficiency for it. If you practice hard enough to where you manage to triple your reading speed, then now is the time for you to apply your new skill into your study habits. However, is there a right way to go about doing so?

Well, yes. Your logic might suggest that since you are now capable of reading three times faster than you used to be able to, then that means that you would be able to read three whole chapters at the same duration it used to take you to read just one chapter. However, this approach wouldn't really be good for learning and recall. Let's say that it used to take you one hour to read one chapter. Now that your reading speed has improved, you shouldn't be trying to fit three whole chapters into that one hour. What you want to do is to read that one chapter three times. This kind of repetitiveness is going to help with recall and retention.

Chapter 8: Accelerated Learning Through Effective Note-taking

Your brain can only absorb so much information in a short amount of time, and that's why it's almost an instinctive process for people to engage in note-taking in a learning session. You can see for yourself whenever you take a look at students in classrooms or office workers in company meetings. However, not a lot of people realize that how they take their notes is very inefficient and actually counterproductive to speedy learning. That doesn't mean to say that note-taking in itself is a faulty learning technique. It's just that there are proper ways to go about it to promote optimized learning and knowledge absorption. That is exactly what this chapter is going to try to highlight. You are going to be equipped with a proper note-taking system that is going to help you grow and develop your knowledge.

Before we focus on the things that you need to do to optimize the note-taking process, it might be good that you are aware of the things that you are doing wrong. A vast majority of people who engage in note-taking make the mistake of just writing down notes purely for the reason of putting words on paper. Most of the time, people do this so that they have a reference to turn back to in the future when they're studying. However, this is a completely incorrect way to go about note-taking. Firstly, it's practically impossible to jot down everything verbatim that a lecturer or a boss might be dictating in a class or a meeting. You are likely to be listening to a 2-hour lecture or a 30-minute meeting. There is no way that you would be able to write everything down. Next, with this method of note-taking, you aren't actively investing yourself in the material that you are jotting down. You are merely putting pen to paper. The process is mostly mechanical and it is almost an entirely mindless activity. You don't really get the chance to analyze the ideas that you are writing down and you fail to implant them in your mind.

The most effective way to go about note-taking would be to always maintain a thinking brain. It can't all be mindless scribbling of random words on a blank piece of paper. You are not a transcriber. You are a learner. As you are paying attention to a source of information such as an audiobook, an educational video, a lecture, or something of the sort, you are going to want to pay attention to the high-level concepts within that source material which you feel like would really help you as a learner. It's okay for you to casually disregard the details that might not be important to your learning process. Here are five efficient and effective note-taking methods as recommended by the website 'Oxford Learning' ("How to Take Study Notes: 5 Effective Note Taking

Methods," 2017).

The Cornell Method

The Cornell method is a common go-to note-taking technique for people who are especially fond of reviewing their notes later on. It is a very clean and structured way to go about note-taking which makes it more convenient for future reference. The whole Cornell method of note-taking is designed to organize your notes into short summaries that are easy to understand.

With the Cornell method, you are going to have to divide the paper which you are taking notes on into three separate sections. A large section at the bottom of the paper should be devoted to the summary. A smaller portion on the left side of the paper should be devoted to cues while a larger portion on the right side of the paper is devoted to the actual notes.

Notes

As you are taking notes in class or a meeting, this is the section where you will want to highlight all the main ideas and concepts that were mentioned. Focus only on the biggest concepts.

Cues

Right after the class or the meeting is over, go over the notes that you made and add specific cues that you can further expound upon once you have additional resources. Add some specific guiding questions or potential references that might help you understand something better.

Summary

In the summary section of your notes, this is where you will want to provide a general overview of everything that you have learned. Focus on only the biggest concepts and highlight the important points that you want to drive home.

The Mapping Method

If you are more of a visual note-taker then this might be the best method for you as far as note-taking is concerned. The Mapping method is designed for you to create a more visual aid that will help you retain the information that you gather during a class, lecture, presentation, or meeting. This is also a great method for when you are forced to relate multiple topics to one another within a single session of note-taking.

The Mapping method can also be considered to be a kind of pyramid format. You have to start with the main topic at the very top of your notes. Then, you slowly branch out to different subtopics as the class or lecture goes on. For every subtopic that you produce, write down the important points or notes that you need to remember or study later on. Repeat this process for the entirety of the session.

The Outlining Method

The Outlining method is one that promotes a very organized and readable presentation of important points and topics that will serve as references for further study. This is especially effective as a means of note-taking for learning sessions or lectures that go into incredible detail about complex topics. It works similarly to the Mapping method but is done in a less visual way with a major emphasis on written words.

In order to effectively make use of the Outlining method, you need to first start with writing the main topic at the very top-left corner of the paper. Then, place the first subtopic just underneath the main topic with a slight indentation towards the right. Under the subtopic, make another indentation for any key points or details that you deem to be important which could supplement the subtopic. Repeat this process for every subtopic that is discussed in the lecture or meeting.

The Charting Method

The Charting method of notetaking incorporates the heavy use of columns in order to neatly structure and organize valuable information. This is also an effective use of note taking for lectures or concepts that have complex connections and relationships with various subtopics.

To properly structure a paper for the Charting method, you are going to want to divide your paper into various columns. In some cases, you might need to make use of extra sheets to accommodate more categories that fall under the main topic. Every time the lecturer or resource material mentions a new category, then devote a new column to that category. Once an important detail or piece of information is mentioned pertaining to a specific category, then list it in the proper column.

The Sentence Method

This method of note-taking might be a little more intensive and it might require more effort than the others, but it's also designed to be more information-centric. It's going to be a lot more detailed, and cover a lot of data quickly. However, it's also going to burn through several sheets of paper as every topic is going to require its own specific page.

To use this method properly, label the top of the paper with a specific category or main idea. Once the resource material displays vital information concerning that topic or category, proceed to write down that point in the form of a complete sentence under that corresponding page.

Chapter 9: Battling Procrastination to Accelerate Learning

A vast majority of people in the world don't know what they need to do in order to learn new concepts in the most efficient and effective means possible. It's very rare for people to know right off the bat which study technique is going to work best for them without trying a bunch of them first. However, it would be unwise to think that people aren't maximizing their capacity to learn just because they are ignorant of various techniques and practices. Rather, one of the most common reasons that people don't get to venture into experiencing various learning techniques is procrastination.

One key tool that you're going to need to productive and efficient with your time as you pursue new skills and disciplines is your ability to combat procrastination. A lot of people are guilty of procrastinating from time to time without even realizing it. That is part of the battle right there; being able to recognize when you're goofing around instead of putting your head down and getting straight to work. Even when you are equipped with all of the most effective accelerated learning techniques in the world, unless you know how to combat procrastination, then you aren't going to be able to find much success in your goals and endeavors.

You have to understand that if you're only going to put in work during the times you feel like doing so, then you aren't going to get too far. If you're only going to go out for a run on the days when you feel like doing so, then it's going to take quite a while before you're actually ready to run a marathon. If you only practice writing on the days when you're inspired to do so, then you probably won't be publishing that novel anytime soon. Sure, you can make use of various accelerated learning techniques to help optimize the learning process. However, if you fail to address the issue of procrastination in your life, then you're still keeping yourself from realizing your full potential as a learner.

According to Margie Warrell, bestselling author and public speaker, procrastination can be very detrimental to a person's overall well-being, and if left unaddressed, could spell some substantial trouble in one's personal life (2013). In a piece that was published by Forbes magazine, Warrell highlighted the importance of always being able to address the triggers of procrastination and understanding why it can be so tempting to just put off work to a later date. There are a number of determinants and factors that could play into a person's decision to procrastinate. A lot of it has to do with insecurity, stress, anxiety, laziness, and maybe even demotivation. However, she says that there is a way to combat procrastination, and it's as simple as following these easy steps:

Establish Your Goal and Give Yourself a Deadline

You just have to establish your goal first. This is where everything is ultimately going to stem from. Sometimes, a lot of people procrastinate and fail to get started purely because they don't know where they are supposed to be headed. That's why you are going to want to be able to set clear directions for yourself. You want to make sure that you have a path that you can follow towards eventual accomplishment and success.

In addition to that, you are also going to want to give yourself a deadline. This is so that you will be able to motivate yourself to keep on pushing forward. It's very easy to slack off whenever you know that there isn't really a sense of urgency just yet. Sometimes, just creating that sense of energy even if it's just within yourself would be enough to get you going.

Break Your Goal Down into Smaller Chunks

Now that you know where the final destination is going to be, it's now important for you to determine what your pit stops for the journey as supposed to be. Break your main goal down into smaller and simpler step. This can make the entire task less intimidating for you. Take it one step at a time if you have to. Remember that small progress is still progress. Every step that you take today is going to be one step further from where you were yesterday. Never underestimate the value of short bursts of effort.

Visualize Your Future Success

Whenever you feel like you want to give up, it's always nice to just think about the future happiness that you would be depriving yourself of if you just choose to slack off. It's very much possible that the stakes won't be so high with your learning. Your career or personal life might not be dependent on whether or not you take the time and effort to actually learn something new or develop proficiency in a skill. It can be so easy to just quit and say that you'll try again at a more convenient time. But you also know that you won't be as happy and as fulfilled as you would be if you actually took the time to and devoted work into mastering these disciplines. You never want the successful version of yourself to exist only in a dream world or ideal scenario. You should envision success for yourself, and want to do whatever you can to manifest that vision into real life.

Turn Your Fear into a Positive

Fear can be a very common cause for people to engage in procrastination. A lot of the time, people will be afraid of trying their hand at something and failing. And so, they resort to never trying anything out at all. However, that can be a very unhealthy way to channel your fear. Perhaps, it might be better to think about just how bad you would feel a few months down the line if you didn't put in the work.

Let Others Hold You Accountable

Communicate your goals to your friends and colleagues. Make sure that they are there to keep you motivated. It's very easy to just give up on something when you know that you are only disappointing yourself. But, if you have other people counting on you to deliver, it can be easier to find motivation to keep on moving and push forward. Allow other people to keep you accountable for your goals. If you say that you want to master the art of playing the guitar, then commit to actually performing a song at your friend's birthday party. This is a great way for you to motivate yourself to learn.

Reward Every Milestone

Don't be afraid of rewarding yourself. If you know that you have done substantial work, then reward yourself with something nice. It doesn't have to be something over-the-top. You just want to make sure that you are able to mark every milestone to create that positive internal dialogue within yourself to keep on pushing forward. When you make it a point to reward yourself for doing good work, you re-energize your spirits and inspire yourself to keep on doing more of the same.

Be Brave and Start Today

As the saying goes, there's no point in waiting to do something tomorrow when you can do it today. Sometimes, there will be days where motivation will be hard to come by. There will be days where your insecurities will be much louder than your inner voice of self-confidence. However, on those days, you're just going to have to fight even harder. Get to work. The hardest part is always the start. Once you get a rhythm going, it will be difficult to stop.

Chapter 10: The Feynman Technique

Richard Feynman is regarded as one of the greatest scientists of the 20th century, and is who the method of accelerated learning is actually inspired by. Even though this particular accelerated learning module is named after him, it's a relatively popular learning tool that a lot of the great thinkers of the world, (Albert Einstein included) have incorporated into their own personal study habits.

"If you can't explain it simply, then you don't understand it well enough."

This is a quote that is commonly attributed to Einstein even though some might say that he never really said or wrote this anywhere. Whatever the case may be, this is essentially the central theme that makes up the Feynman technique. It is actually a learning tool that is designed for the learner not just to master a specific topic or discipline, but also to master the teaching of this skill or discipline to another person. It's essentially forcing oneself to learn something in-depth in order to effectively communicate it to another person.

How does this all work out? Well, this chapter is going to be dedicated to teaching you the art of learning through teaching. This is precisely what the

Feynman technique is all about. It is a learning method that is designed to help improve your ability to recall complex concepts and memorize important points. It's going to help you organize and structure your thoughts in an orderly fashion and aid in developing your self-awareness so that you are better able to spot gaps in your logic and your understanding of a certain topic. It's also a very practical and fulfilling way to go about learning something new.

The Feynman Technique can essentially be fulfilled in just 7 simple steps:

Identify the Main Topic and Write Down Everything You Know About It

This is the very first thing that you will want to do because you are going to want to really test your knowledge on the topic firsthand. You don't want to take a linear approach to learning something if you already know a lot on this topic already. If you're building a house, and you see a problem with the flooring on the second floor, that doesn't mean that you need to break down the entire first floor as well. The point of this first phase is for you to see what you know in order to make yourself more aware of what you don't know.

Take One Concept from Your List and Expand on it Using Your Stock Knowledge

Once you have laid everything out on the table, then you can proceed to actually expand on main ideas and concepts even further. Take a step by step approach to it by focusing on a single concept at a time. Jot down every single point or piece of information that you might have in your brain that could help you enforce your main concepts. This is where you really go into detail about everything that you may know in connection with the main topic.

Imagine Teaching or Presenting These Topics to Other People

Once you feel like you have already exhausted all of your knowledge on paper, then it might be time to actually pretend teaching this topic to an imaginary audience. Try presenting everything that you know to the walls of a private room where it's just yourself and a bunch of imaginary people. Make it as legitimate a presentation as possible. Really put everything you have into it. Make it seem like your imaginary audience is really yearning to learn more about this topic from you and relying on you to deliver on that front.

Identify the Potential Problem Areas in Which You Have Trouble Explaining

If you aren't truly a master of the topic just yet, it's likely that you will find many gaps in logic and problem areas that will require fixing. This is essentially the problem finding aspect of the learning process. You will want to figure out where all of your weak points are so that you will know which areas you will have to focus on improving in your learning process. This is now the part where you are looking for cracks on the wall, leaks in the roof, and the faults in the wiring of your home.

Go Back and Fill in the Gaps and then Repeat Step 2 and 3

Once you have successfully figured out where the problem areas are, it's now time for you to take action. Refer to any reliable source materials or seek the help of a mentor in order for you to fill in those gaps and become more confident with your knowledge of a certain topic. Refine your presentation even further by repeating steps 2 and 3 of the process so long as it is necessary.

Simplify Your Presentation Even Further by Using Analogies

When you are confident about all of the knowledge you have acquired and the research that you have done to be a master in this particular field of study, it is now time to simplify your thoughts and ideas even further. The reason that you want to simplify your thoughts is because you want to make sure that you understand these concepts in their simplest form. If you are able to incorporate analogies into your presentation of ideas, then that is further affirmation of the solid grasp that you might have over these points and ideas.

If You are Willing, Try Teaching the Concept to Others

This last step isn't really a necessary one, but if you're feeling brave enough, you can go ahead and actually try teaching other people about the topic. It's always nice whenever you are able to put yourself out there and really test your knowledge. This is also an opportunity for you to gather valuable feedback from other people who would be able to give you an outsider's perspective of the way that you present your ideas. If they see any potential weak points, then you would be able to defend it or take it as a learning opportunity. Either way, you strengthen your understanding of the subject even further.

Chapter 11: Learning Through Listening

Again, whenever someone wants to learn more about a particular topic or field of study, it's completely normal for one to gravitate towards a textbook or some kind of reading material. However, it's also very common for people to attend lectures or listen to presentations in an effort to acquire knowledge about a specific field of interest. You might be a businessman who has gone off to a conference in an effort to learn more about sales techniques or management tactics. You might be a college student who is attending a lecture with a professor who doesn't make use of slides or visual aids. It's during situations like these where you will really have to rely on your listening skills in order for you to accelerate your learning within these specific scenarios.

According to Lee and Hatesohl from the University of Missouri, studies indicate that out of the total communication time that a human being allots in a day, 45% of that time is devoted purely to listening (1993). However, studies also show that the average human being's listening technique is flawed and inefficient.

Why are we so bad at listening?

You're hearing me, but you're not listening. That's a phrase that often gets said a lot. That is essentially the whole brunt of the issue right there. Just because you hear someone saying a bunch of words, phrases, and sentences to you doesn't mean that you are necessarily listening to them. That is exactly the point that this chapter is going to focus on. You are going to learn more about why the way that you listen is wrong, and why you aren't really learning efficiently with your method of listening. Also, you are going to learn about proper listening techniques that you can adopt as one of your personal learning habits.

However, before you can figure out what it is you need to do to improve the way that you listen to others, it's important that you first understand what you're doing wrong in the first place.

You don't listen to what you're not interested in

Picture this scenario for a little bit. You are a college student, and you know that you hate mathematics. You go out of your way to avoid any majors that might require you to do any mathematical problems. You opt for a degree in liberal arts or music instead. But then, when you take a look at your syllabus, you notice that there are a few units of math that you need to take.

So, you reluctantly go to class, and you try to listen as your mathematics professor explains formulas, equations, and more. However, you can't seem to grasp anything, because you don't really see the value of learning it in the first place. You go into the learning process with such a negative disposition that you are practically crippling yourself and your capacity to learn. Sometimes, you just have to try to make an effort to actually listen to something even though you might not be entirely interested in it.

You criticize the messenger, but not the message

Don't miss the whole point of the lecture or a class that you're in. You are there to learn about a particular topic. You're not there to learn about the speaker or the lecturer themselves. If you are too fixated on what the lecturer is wearing or the manner in which they are speaking, then you risk completely distracting yourself from the true goal of attending the lecture in the first place. Sometimes, you can get too sidetracked by your perception of the lecturer to the point that the actual message of the lecture becomes completely irrelevant. Always make sure that when you are listening, pay attention to the message, and not the messenger.

You tolerate a lot of distractions

Put your cell phone on vibrate mode and make sure to keep them tucked away in your bag until the lecture is over. If someone you find attractive is seated right beside you, then consider just moving to another seat if you feel like you can't keep yourself from getting distracted. Sometimes, you can become overly stimulated by things that have nothing to do with the actual lecture itself and you end up missing out on some valuable points or bits of information. You really have to make sure that you stay focused on the task at hand. Your brain can only accommodate so many stimulants at once.

You try to elude difficult and challenging topics

If you only ever really pay attention to the people who have nice and easy-to-understand things to say to you, then you're never really going to learn much from listening at all. The whole point of accelerated learning through listening is exposing yourself to difficult or challenging topics that you might not know much about. That's the essence of learning in any medium. So, don't shut yourself off from listening to someone just because you know that it's going to be difficult for you to understand. Always take every learning opportunity that you can and try to make the most out of them.

You let your emotions get the best of you

There are plenty of times during the course of a speech or a lecture where the speaker might tap into the feelings or emotions of the audience. Even though it might be tempting to let your emotions get the best of you and allow yourself to be swayed by the energy or charisma of the speaker, you have to resist that temptation. You can't let your feelings compromise the level of learning that could potentially be taking place. Always try to maintain as objective a viewpoint as possible. Don't let your feelings cloud your judgment or analysis of a point.

You stick to only one viewpoint

It's not enough that you are making an effort to hear out the person who is speaking right in front of you. It's also just as important that you make an effort to stay open-minded. You might not necessarily believe or agree with what the person is saying, but the whole point of listening is to try to learn something new from someone. That means that you are bound to listen to a few things that might not resonate with your own belief system. Reserve your judgment for the very end. You may risk missing out on a very important and valuable point because you are too engrossed in your own thoughts and belief systems.

How do we improve our listening to accelerate learning?

Fortunately, there is a way you can go about improving the way that you listen to people. It's all just a matter of employing at least one or a healthy combination of all three of these techniques the next time you are listening to someone give a presentation or a speech. It's true when they say that people do too much talking in this world, but not enough listening. Remember that when you are talking, you are essentially reinforcing to yourself and to other people what you think you already know. But when you take the time to listen, you are giving yourself an opportunity to expand your worldview and your perspective on things. That is why a good listener is going to be more adept at learning than a good talker.

Go to Where You Think the Speaker is going

Instead of being reactionary with your listening, try being a proactive listener instead. What does this mean? Usually, when you're listening to someone speak, you might have a tendency to engage in passive listening. This means that you let them do all of the talking, and you just absorb and react off what they feed you. But with proactive listening, you are actually trying to beat them to the punch. Instead of waiting for the speaker to hand you the main point on a silver platter, try getting there yourself before you even give them a chance to do so. This proactive method of listening really engages your mind and primes it to be able to absorb new concepts and information better.

Focus on the Supporting Points or Arguments

When someone tells you that cutting down on the consumption of red meat is going to be good for you, it's not really that interesting of a point that would compel or sway you. However, if someone tells you that the consumption of red meat is good for you because it helps lower the levels of cholesterol and blood pressure in your body, then the point immediately becomes more compelling. Why? It's because the main point is only reinforced further by a supporting point or argument. When you are listening to someone, don't fixate on a main point. Instead, pay attention to all the supporting points and arguments instead. Once you are able to substantiate a main point, it becomes a lot easier to understand, memorize, and communicate to others later on.

Make Note of Mental Summaries As You Are Listening

If you are listening to a speaker or a lecturer, it's very unlikely that they are going to go on and on with their lecture without stopping or having few pauses here and there. These pauses might not be too long, but they are still going to serve as opportunities for you to make short summaries of what they might have just said. It's a great way for you to understand what the speaker is trying to convey, and it's also an effective way to bring about retention and recall for these particular topics and concepts.

Chapter 12: Experiential Learning

Just by looking at its name, the method of experiential learning should really be self-explanatory. It is essentially an accelerated learning technique that enforces the idea of learning through actual experience. Famed and accomplished psychologists John Dewey and Jean Piaget are often credited for being the fathers of experiential learning. But, many key figures in the scientific community will agree that it was the work of David A. Kolb, an educational theorist and professor of Organizational Behavior, that really brought the subject of experiential learning into the mainstream.

Many scientists, theorists, and educators have made use of this transformative method of education and learning through various experiments, tests, and actual classroom applications. All in all, it is a very immersive form of education as it leans heavily on the learner's actual experience of a concept or an idea, and not just a theoretical understanding of it. This entire chapter is going to be dedicated to promoting the idea of experiential learning as a great tool in order to accelerate one's understanding or absorption of a complex task or idea. You are going to be briefed on the various reasons on why experiential learning is actually a great way to learn.

You will also be given practical insight into how you can make use of experiential learning to speed up your development and mastery of a particular discipline.

Reasons Why Experiential Learning is a Transformative Form of Learning

Rajiv Jayaraman, the CEO and founder of employee development solutions firm KNOLSKAPE, shared his thoughts on experiential learning and its value on human development in a blog post. He claimed that experiential learning is the best way to combat the increasing likelihood of attention deficiency and personal disinterest or detachment in the contemporary learner. In the article that he wrote, he highlighted 8 specific reasons as to why experiential learning is actually a groundbreaking form of learning (2014).

It Accelerates Learning

Experiential learning is a much more efficient and effective way to get a person to really learn something. Repetitive learning or the method of learning by sheer repetition has proven to be very inefficient and just downright boring for a lot of people. With experiential learning, the learner is actually enticed and motivated to engage in critical thinking, problem solving, and decision-making. The immersive and intuitive experience speeds up the learning process even more.

It Offers a Comfortable and Safe Learning Environment

Experiential learning is a really great way to offer a learner an opportunity to actually learn and put valuable life skills to use in a safe and controlled environment. For example, when teaching a small child the basics of human body mechanics, you can bring him or her to a small playground to actually use their body to traverse various terrain and obstacles. The child is offered an opportunity to learn how to use their bodies through actual experience, but is still provided safety, security, comfort, and supervision.

It Increases a Person's Level of Engagement

There is just a higher level of focus, engagement, and collaboration whenever a learner is forced to undergo an experiential lesson. Senses are heightened and one's mind is definitely sharpened and primed to engage in an immersive learning experience as a result of sensory overload. There is also a higher level of emotional investment on the part of the learner whenever they fully engage themselves with the task or challenge at hand. Being thrust straight into the middle of the experience is definitely somewhat of an eye-opener, and it can demand one's full focus and attention.

It Helps Bridge the Gap Between Theory and Practice

In more traditional methods of learning, it would be the teacher, mentor, or lecturer explaining concepts and ideas in theoretical form. However, experiential learning is able to bridge the gap between the formality of theoretical education and practical application. A learner is no longer left to comprehend thoughts and ideas without actually getting an opportunity to experience them firsthand. With experiential learning, it is a healthy merge of both learning processes.

It Produces Dramatic Changes in Mindset

Whenever a human being undergoes an impactful or dramatic experience, it can really trigger a drastic change in one's mindset. The effects of learning by experience are much more profound than just learning theory alone. Not to say that listening to a life-changing lecture from a world-class speaker wouldn't produce dramatic results or changes in mindset. It's just that this form of learning would be largely dependent on the content of the lecture and the lecturer themselves. With experiential learning, the dramatic changes come as a direct result of the module or training methodology.

It Delivers Excellent Return on Investment

The act of teaching and learning is an investment. As a teacher, you are investing yourself in the learner. As a learner, you are investing in the learning material and yourself. That is why you are always going to want to make sure that you are making the proper investments in the right methodologies. Experiential learning offers a great return on investment because of the growth and development that a learner gains from the entire training methodology.

It Provides Accurate Assessment Results

With theoretical learning, it can be very hard to gauge or assess the growth and development of the learner. Theoretical testing can only provide theoretical assessments which will not necessarily translate into real-life application. However, with experiential learning, it can be much easier to accurately gauge the progress and development of a learner. For example, testing a programming student's ability to recall various algorithms and commands is completely different from having a student build an entire program from scratch with set specifications. Experiential learning focuses more on the application of theories than just the theories in themselves.

It Enables Personalized Learning

Experiential learning always offers a personalized learning experience for the student. It's never really a one-size-fits-all kind of learning methodology because everyone is going to have different preferences, tastes, dispositions, and personalities. Experiential learning understands that everyone learns in very different ways. This means that it's important to assess, design, derive, guide, and mentor each learner in a very personalized manner. This is something that experiential learning is going to be able to provide both the learner and the mentor.

Chapter 13: The Method of Loci - A Memory Technique

The method of loci isn't necessarily a revolutionary method of learning or memorization as it is a technique that has been around for centuries. It is essentially a memorization technique that revolves around attaching or attributing particular points of interests to familiar routes that you take on a consistent basis. This is a method of learning or memorization that is particularly effective for people who need to memorize long lists that they might typically be unfamiliar with. This entire chapter is going to brief you on a short history on the origins of the method along with a few tips and tricks on how you can use the method in your daily life.

Origins

It is very difficult to pinpoint the exact origins of the method of loci as it is indeed one of the oldest memory techniques in the history of civilization. However, it is widely believed that it was in Cicero's 'De Oratore' where the concept was first put into formal writing. In Cicero's work, he attributed the invention of the method of loci to the Greek philosopher and poet Simonides. In his recount of the story, Cicero claims that Simonides managed to escape a burning building that was hosting a lavish party for the most affluent and notable people of the time in that area. Simonides took it upon himself to try to identify the bodies of the burnt victims after the tragedy, and he invented the method of loci in an effort to recall who those people were.

Instead of analyzing the burnt cadavers themselves, Simonides instead tried to recall where certain people were seated and situated during the party in order to identify where their burnt bodies had ended up. Legend says that this is exactly how the method of loci was born. This is why the method of loci is more commonly known as the *memory palace* or *mind palace* which has often been referenced in the BBC's television rendition of the classic Sherlock Holmes.

How It Works

Essentially, in order for you to use the method of loci in your own life, you must first visualize a familiar route, room, or location that you know by heart. Perhaps, you can envision your own bedroom, your entire house, your college campus, or even your daily route to work. Whatever route you choose, it's important that you make sure that this is always going to be the route that you use whenever you employ this technique. Once you have chosen a route, you must then identify important landmarks or points in the route which can serve as representations for the ideas or concepts that you want to memorize. If you have chosen your bedroom as your memory palace, then you might want to consider your bed to be the first landmark, your television set as the second, and then your bookcase as the third, and so on... The point is that you have to establish a sequential order that you can go back to consistently.

If you are tasked with memorizing the first five presidents of the United States, then you have to designate each character to the first five landmarks or route points that you have set for yourself in your memory palace. In order to do so, you must first research and read up on who the first five presidents are:

George Washington - John Adams - Thomas Jefferson - James Madison - James Monroe

Let's say that you use your house as your memory palace for this particular exercise. You must now determine which landmarks in your house that you're going to use. Ideally, you will want to designate your landmarks in an intuitive, sequential order. Since you wake up in your bedroom every morning, the first landmark of your home could be your bedroom, and maybe you make it a habit of going to the bathroom right away whenever you wake up. The bathroom could be the second landmark. After using the bathroom, you might have to walk down to the kitchen using the stairs so you can have some breakfast. The stairs could be the third landmark. Before entering the kitchen, you have to walk through the living room. The living room can serve as the fourth landmark. Finally, the kitchen can serve as the fifth and final landmark. So, the order of your landmarks would be as follows:

Bedroom - Bathroom - Stairs - Living Room - Kitchen

As you visualize yourself making your way through your house, you have to then attribute each landmark to the president that you have to memorize. When you envision yourself in your bedroom, think of George Washington being there. When you walk into your bathroom, think of John Adams, and so on. Ideally, you will want to attribute each character to something that relates to them within every landmark. In your bedroom, you might have a book about George Washington's life in there somewhere which you can use as a link. In the bathroom, you can think of *the John* which is a British way of referring to the bathroom. It's not necessary that you make use of memory techniques like this, but it does help with one's ability to retain vital information.

General Rules and Guidelines

As simple as the method of loci might be, there are still certain rules or guidelines that you are going to want to stick to in order to really make the most out of this methodology.

The route you choose must be one that is very familiar to you

The method of loci won't work if you aren't familiar with the route that you will choose for your memory palace. It has to be a route or a location that you would know practically by heart. If you have trouble remembering the specifics of the route or location that you choose, then it would probably compromise the entire methodology as a whole.

Each landmark within that route must always be distinct and unique

It's very important that every designated landmark or pit stop in the route is unique and distinct. This is because if two or more points in the route are rather similar and indistinguishable, there is a chance that you will end up confusing yourself when trying to recall the proper attributions and representations that you set in your head. For example, if you use your college campus as your designated route for your mind palace, then it might not be a good idea to designate two identical classrooms as two separate points in the route. Make sure to mix it up by using offices, libraries, gyms, laboratories, and so on.

You must follow the same order of the route every single time

You have to think of your memory as a muscle. The more consistently that you work your muscles and put them to use, the stronger they become. This is exactly how the method of loci works. The more you use this methodology as a means of memorizing something, then the more proficient you will become at memory and information retention. That is why it's always ideal that you would make use of the same route and landmarks every single time you try to use this method. Remember that consistency breeds efficiency.

Get creative with your attributions and representations

The more effort you put into getting creative with how you represent certain characters, items, or ideas, then the easier it will be for you to actually remember these things. This is because you are immersing and investing yourself more and more into the memory technique, and that means that you are activating your mind more efficiently.

Chapter 14: Efficient Cramming for an Exam

When you are in school, you are always told that it's a bad idea to cram for your tests, examinations, and projects. Your teacher tells you that you are always given sufficient time to prepare for an exam, and you should make the most out of that time in its entirety. You shouldn't wait until the very last minute before you start the preparation process. You are constantly reminded to stay ahead of your work so that you never have to end up playing catch-up with your tasks and projects. However, there is no denying that a lot of us have procrastinated at one point or another. In fact, a lot of us only ever resort to procrastination whenever we are given things to do. This chapter is going to be dedicated to people who constantly find themselves having to cram for an exam or a test.

Granted, it's important to preface the rest of this chapter with the reminder that it's always important that you give yourself ample time to prepare for an examination. The best way to accelerate your learning is to make sure that you give yourself the time to do things properly. Ideally, you would still want to do everything that you can to stop putting yourself in positions to cram and rush the preparation process. However, it's understandable that there will be instances where you won't have the time to do things far in advance. You might have too many things on your plate, and so you have to deprioritize studying. In those cases, it might be good to make use of the techniques that will be highlighted in this chapter. But again, it's important to only use cramming as a last resort. It shouldn't be your go-to method for preparing for examinations and tests. You might not necessarily get the best grades in your class with this method, but it could make the difference between you getting a passing grade or a failing one.

In this chapter, we are going to refer to various key figures who have written valuable resource materials on the matter. Blogger and learning expert David Pierce, wrote extensively in a blog post for GearFire about the best way to approach cramming the night before an exam. We are also going to touch on points made by Skylar Anderson in an article that he wrote for the StudyRight website. Again, both resource writers emphasize that cramming should only ever be a last resort in an emergency situation. It shouldn't be a consistent practice for anyone who wants to achieve high grades. Here are a few tips that you will want to consider in order to really be efficient in the way that you cram.

Prepare All of the Study Materials that You Need

There's no time for you to be going back and forth from the library and your house for any books or resource materials that you might need as you begin the cramming process. Before you even start, you have to make sure that you already have all of the materials that you might need. This means that you have to prepare all the books, references, your calculator, ruler, pens, pencils, papers, laptop, and everything even before you sit down and flip a page. Once you begin the process of cramming, you don't want to keep on getting up to grab something. Expect to be seated for a prolonged period of time, which brings us to the next tip...

Find a Spot with Minimal Distractions Where You Can Sit for an Extended Period of Time

Again, once you sit down, expect to stay there until you finish. There is no time for you to keep on transferring from one study spot to another. Decide on one place and stick to it. Make sure that you choose a spot that has minimal distractions. You can choose to lock yourself in your study or in your bedroom. You can go to a library that will accommodate you for plenty of hours. You can visit a coffee shop that won't be closing its doors anytime soon. Whatever the case, make sure that you pick a spot that you won't have to get up and move from for the entire duration of the cramming process.

Excuse Yourself from the Social Media World

Social media has proven itself to be one of the greatest distractions of the 21st century. Yes, it does a great job of connecting people to one another, and it's really a great resource for collaboration and social interaction, but you don't have the luxury of time for you to be engaging in any social media at this point. You will want to minimize distractions as much as possible. If you have to temporarily deactivate your Facebook, Instagram, and Twitter accounts for the meantime, then you should do so. You should only ever really be using the internet to gather more information about a certain topic.

Make Use of the 50/10 Principle

Just because it was mentioned that you're going to be seated for an extended period of time doesn't mean that you should be studying for multiple hours on end without stopping. Yes, you are under the pressure of time right now, but you have to understand your limitations. Your brain can only handle and process so much information at a time. It can even get to a point where your brain will be overworked and your studying becomes slow and inefficient. That's why it's a good idea to give yourself breaks every so often just to reset and refresh your brain. A common practice that people make use of while cramming is the 50/10 principle. In a span of 60 minutes, you are going to want to spend 50 minutes purely studying, and use the final 10 minutes to do whatever you want just to refresh your brain. Repeat this process for as long as necessary.

Fuel Up on Caffeine

A lot of people are going to be skeptical of caffeine for its potentially harmful effects on the human body, but there are also going to be those who will defend the value of caffeine especially while cramming. However, when you are in the process of cramming, your perceived notion of health might have to take a backseat for purposes of preparation. A little caffeine isn't going to do you any substantial harm. You are going to want to do whatever you can to stay alert, awake, and focused for an extended amount of time without completely compromising your health. This is exactly what caffeine is going to be able to do for you. Consistent caffeine use might potentially be bad for a person's health, especially when heart conditions are involved. However, occasional caffeine consumption should be fine, especially when you need the extra energy to get something done.

Focus on the Big Ideas and Rewrite

You don't have much time at this point. This means that you can't really be going into detail when reviewing or reading your notes. You are only going to have enough time to focus on the big ideas. This should be sufficient enough to get you a decent score. The best way to go about remembering these important points is to rewrite them into a new set of notes that you can use later on for review or reference. When you take the time to understand and rewrite these big concepts onto a new set of notes, then you are reinforcing your understanding of these concepts. For more help on note taking while cramming, feel free to go back to Chapter 8 of this book.

Recruit All of Your Senses

At the risk of sounding and looking crazy to the people around you, you are going to want to recruit the use of all of your senses while you are cramming. Sensory overload is a great and effective way to immerse yourself fully in what you are doing. That means if you make the most out of all your senses while you are studying, you are investing more of your mind and energy into what you are doing. When reading an important concept, try saying it out loud to yourself. Incorporate physical gestures and hand movements as you stress important points. These techniques can all aid in your ability to retain and recall information.

Find a Study Buddy

Collaborative learning is always going to prove to be a more efficient method of learning as opposed to solo-studying. According to Career Step, an online platform for career-focused education and training, having compatible study buddies will always prove to be more beneficial to a learner than studying alone (2014). Ben Hartman, the Director of Admissions at Career Step, says that having a study buddy is a more enriching and fulfilling way to enhance the learning experience as a whole. If you are cramming, it might do you good to recruit the help of someone who is studying for the same exam. You can help test one another and the camaraderie gives you an extra boost to study harder.

Make Use of the Chunking Technique

Try memorizing the first 10 digits of pi:

3.141592653

Not so easy, is it? But what if you try segmenting it this way:

3.14 - 159 - 26 - 53

Instead of memorizing the entire value of pi as a whole, you can try to break it down into different chunks so that you will be able to memorize it better. This is the memorization technique that is commonly referred to as 'chunking'. You take a big concept or an idea and you break it down into smaller chunks that are easier to absorb. Breaking down your syllabus is also going to be less intimidating than having to absorb everything in one go.

Reward Yourself

Reward yourself every so often. It can be very disheartening to know that you have so much information that you need to absorb within a short span of time. However, if you positively reinforce yourself in the form of incentives and rewards, it can be very easy to find the motivation that you need to keep on going until you're done. Maybe you can reward yourself with a bite of your chocolate bar for every chapter that you finish reading through. Sometimes, you just need to incentivize yourself in simple ways to get the motivation going.

Get Some Sleep

Lastly, you are going to want to make sure that you get some sleep. There's no point in pulling an all-nighter if your brain is going to be too tired on exam day to be able to recall everything that you've crammed. Sleep is a great way for your mind to repair and recover from a hectic cram session. You want your mind to be extremely alert on the day of the examination. That's why you need to allot some time for sleep.

Chapter 15: Collaborative Learning in a Group Setting

In a nutshell, collaborative learning is a learning theory that proposes the idea of group learning as being a more efficient methodology than solitary studying. It is a learning environment that encourages collaborative efforts from several individuals who share a singular goal. It is where learners are designed to work together in an effort to understand a certain concept or solve a shared problem. This chapter is going to delve deeper into what the benefits of collaborative learning are as opposed to other traditional methods of learning. It is also going to brief you on the proper ways to go about collaborative learning to yield the highest possible return on investments.

Benefits of Collaborative Learning

A collaborative learning system is one that encourages joint scholarly effort on the part of multiple invested parties. Each learner might have unique and specific motivations that drive them to learn or study a particular topic. However, they all share the same goals in the eventual mastery and development of a particular skill or discipline. Some of the benefits of collaborative learning include:

It helps enhance the problem-solving process

Collaborative learning is known to improve one's problem-solving capabilities. In a collaborative learning setting, students are brought together by a shared goal that they set for themselves. This means that these learners are also going to share similar challenges, hurdles, and problems on their way to achieving the goals that they have. When there is greater collaboration in the discussion, analysis, and approach towards solving these problems, it helps develop the individual's capacity to overcome adversity and challenges as well. A lot of the time solitary learners can feel defeated and discouraged when having to face adversity, but with the power of a group behind them, it can be easier for one to feel confident about addressing certain problems and issues.

It induces a higher form of critical thinking

There is always going to be a greater pressure to analyze, deconstruct, clarify, or reinforce certain topics and subject matters whenever you are in a collaborative learning environment. Your senses are always going to be heightened and overloaded due to the increased stimulation brought about by your learning peers. This means that you would end up paying better attention and giving more effort to the analysis of the topics being discussed. You are already priming your senses to engage in intense levels of critical thinking and analysis whenever there is a group component to it.

It improves one's social skills

Solitary learning is fine especially if people are able to find substantial success in it. However, there is one valuable skill that one is typically deprived of whenever they engage in mere solitary learning as opposed to collaborative learning: social development. In life, there is no escaping the value of having developed social skills. That's why collaborative learning is a more holistic approach to learning or mastering a certain subject or field. It never negates the social aspect of learning, and so it ends up being a better-rounded approach to learning as a whole.

It encourages accountability in learning

Holding yourself accountable to your learning isn't always going to be as compelling as when other people hold you accountable. You might set a certain deadline for yourself to learn how to play guitar on your own, but it can be very easy to just abandon that deadline when the only person you are accountable to is yourself. At the end of the day, you only end up disappointing yourself, and it can be very easy to just restart your efforts with minimal consequences. However, it's a completely different story whenever other people hold you accountable.

Let's say that you are a member of a band, and all of you are tasked to learn how to play a particular song with your own specific instruments. This is a collaborative learning environment where all of you share a unified goal to develop your skill and mastery for a particular song. If you fail to do your part, then you are essentially disappointing and invalidating the efforts of your bandmates in the process. Having a group of people to hold you accountable for your efforts can be very effective in actually motivating you to exert more effort into your practice.

It develops a person's communication skills

A lot of the time, your mastery of a certain concept or idea is only as good as your ability to communicate it to other people in an effective manner. There is no point in you mastering the art of business leadership and organizational management if you aren't able to communicate these points to people who would most benefit from it. That is why the development of your communication skills is going to be just as important as your mastery in complex concepts and specialized topics. When you are forced to learn a discipline within the context of a group, you will also be forced to develop your communication skills as well. This is going to be an aspect of your learning that you will be forced not to neglect.

It fosters diversity and open-mindedness

One of the most important traits that a person needs to develop to maximize one's capacity to learn is open-mindedness. This is a trait that is emphasized and takes center stage in a collaborative learning environment. When you're studying on your own, you only have your own perspective and understanding to work with. If you are working within the confines of a group, you have the luxury of being able to consult the understandings and perspectives of other people in order to further sharpen your own understanding of a matter.

It accelerates learning

That's the whole point of this book, isn't it? It's all about accelerating one's learning, and that is exactly what collaborative learning would be able to gift its learners. A lot of the time, solitary learners can encounter some huge mental blocks and intellectual hurdles that can slow them down and impede their progress. You might have already encountered this problem in the past with your own study experiences. You find yourself reading a segment of a textbook over and over again because you can't seem to understand it. If you are studying as a part of a group, there is likely someone within your group who has a better grasp or understanding of a concept. They would then be able to help you understand something better, and it would minimize the negative effects of experiencing mental blockages.

At the same time, if you know that you have a good understanding of a complex topic that another person in the group is struggling with, you will have an opportunity to further reinforce your understanding of that topic by explaining it to your study peer. Either way, you can dramatically benefit from being able to collaborate with someone else as you are studying or mastering a new discipline.

Chapter 16: Binaural Beats for Effective Studying

Think back to the many times in your life where you sat down at a desk ready to get to work and learn something new. You open the page of a textbook or you go to a website with valuable resource materials. A couple of lines in, you're doing fine, but then, suddenly, your mind randomly drifts towards different thoughts and ideas that have nothing to do with what you're trying to learn and study at all. This all confuses you, and you're frustrated at yourself. You try to power through and you read through the entire page from start to finish. What do you have to show for yourself? Nothing. You don't remember or understand a single thing. So, you find yourself starting from the top.

Haven't you ever wondered why this happens to you? Haven't you ever thought about why your brain just refuses to cooperate sometimes? Well, the answer is pretty simple and straightforward. The reason you find your mind drifting away off to places you don't want it to go is because you haven't primed it for focused learning.

Think of your mind as the gearbox of a car. You can put your mind in neutral, in drive, in park, or in reverse. If you want your mind to focus on a specific task, it's important that you are first able to put it into the right gear. Like a car, your mind needs to be in the proper gear in order for it to do what you want it to do. You can't expect to propel your car forward if you put the gear into neutral. It's exactly the same way with your mind. You can't expect your mind to focus on learning if it's stuck on wandering and exploration.

So, how exactly do you put your mind into the right gear? It's not like there's a particular button you can press to put it into learning mode, is there? Well, it turns out that there very well may be.

This is where the concept of binaural beats comes in. This chapter is going to focus on how binaural beats can help put your mind into the proper headspace to learn efficiently and effectively. However, before we can do that, it's important that you first gain a simple understanding of your brain works.

The Mechanics of the Mind

You need to be able to think of your brain as a very complex machine that is composed of a very complicated web of cells that are referred to as neurons. The neurons in your brain are primarily responsible for transmitting data and information to and from the various parts of your brains. When your neurons are functioning properly, they produce a certain level of electrical energy depending on the stage of their activity.

When your brain is firing on all cylinders and becoming hyperactive, it emerges into what is called the Beta state. This is when your neurons are exhibiting high levels of activity. Gradually, as the activity levels in your brain slows down and your neurons are more subdued, your brain enters into its Alpha state. Ultimately, when the brain powers down into a low-functioning mode, the kind you get into when you fall asleep, it is referred to as the Delta state.

That is the extent of your required understanding of cranial functions for you to understand how binaural beats work. Just know that your brain doesn't learn well when it is in its hyperactive or Beta state. It is also virtually incapable of absorbing information when it is in its low-power or Delta state. Your brain is most primed for learning whenever it falls into its Alpha state.

Binaural beats are essentially a tool that you can use to induce your brain into entering an Alpha state.

The Impediments of Focus

Why is it that you often find your brain in a Beta state and how do you transition it into an Alpha state instead? Well, there are many determinants that factor into whether your brain is in a Beta state or not. However, ultimately, the answer lies in the level of stress and anxiety that you have in your life. The more anxious that you feel at any given moment, the more that you are feeding into the Beta state of your brain. This is why it's always a lot harder for you to focus on your studying or learning whenever you are in a state of anxiety or stress. Your brain is in a hyperactive state, and that can make it challenging for new information to be absorbed and stored.

Putting your brain into a Beta state is going to require a lot of energy, and that's why your brain can feel really exhausted whenever you feel stressed and overwhelmed with things that are taking place in your life. You might be sitting down in a comfortable chair, but if you feel stressed, it can leave you feeling physically tired and exhausted. In order for you to really focus on a task at hand, you have to be able to induce an Alpha state in your brain. But how do you go about doing so?

Getting to Alpha through Binaural Beats

It's going to be difficult for anyone to achieve a mental state of Alpha left to his or her own devices. The challenge of achieving Alpha only intensifies when you feel an immense amount of stress or pressure in your life. However, it turns out that there is a really simple solution to alleviating that stress and pressure in your life to Alpha quickly and easily: music.

Binaural beats are essentially imaginary beats that are perceived by your brain whenever it is forced to comprehend two different frequencies that are being pushed into each ear. Binaural beats are most effective whenever the user or learner is wearing stereo headphones.

If one ear is being fed a sound frequency of 110hz and the other ear is being fed a frequency of 100hz, then the brain is instinctively going to create an artificial sound of 10hz in order to compensate for the difference. In order to feel the full effects of binaural beats, you are going to want to listen to two separate frequencies with a difference of around 8hz-12hz. When you engage in listening to binaural beats, your brain slowly transitions into a state of Alpha and is primed to focus on a specific task.

The Science and Sensation of Listening to Binaural Beats

According to a study that was published in the Frontiers of Psychiatry Journal, binaural beats can actually have dramatic effects on one's cognitive and analytical skills (Chaieb, Wilpert, Reber, & Fell, 2015). Whenever you make use of binaural beats, your brain automatically shifts into a gear of focus and concentration. It helps in calming your nerves and anxieties, therefore reinforcing your brain's capacity to entertain and absorb new information. It induces a state of calm in your mind that is just enough to cultivate a conducive state for learning without making one sleepy or drowsy. Activities like meditation or yoga are also known to induce a state of Alpha in the brain.

However, it is important to note that using binaural beats for focus and concentration is most effective when making use of stereo headphones that are able to cancel or block out external noise. It's absolutely essential that each ear is able to distinguish the difference in frequency of the sound that is being fed into each of them.

It might also be important to note that people who are epileptic or pregnant should first consult a physician prior to engaging in binaural beat meditation or listening. Listening to binaural beats is a typically safe activity, however, it can possibly induce seizures in people who are epileptic.

There is a vast availability of binaural beats out there on various media platforms such as YouTube or Spotify. They are fairly simple to produce and they don't really require much analysis or attention. It's as simple as putting your headphones on and pressing play. Boom. Instant focus.

Chapter 17: Flashcards for Effective Studying

You see this study tool all the time in television shows and movies that depict montages of kids studying for tests and exams. It's a very common tool that is widely used by people all over the world regardless of culture, background, or subject matter. All sorts of people, ranging from a little girl studying for her 3rd-grade math exam to the high-powered CEO preparing for a big company presentation to the board, make use of this age-old tool for studying and recall: the flashcard.

Flashcards are a relatively simple tool, and yet, they are so incredibly effective in helping people achieve something called 'active recall' - a common tool or practice that accelerates learning. This chapter is going to highlight just how effective flashcards can be to promote accelerated learning, while also developing your understanding of how you can best utilize them in your study endeavors.

The flashcard system is a relatively simple one to grasp. On one side of the card, you place an important question that is connected to what you are studying. On the opposite side of that same card, you will have to place your answer. Making use of flashcards is a transformative way of testing yourself while also familiarizing yourself with the study material at the same time.

Common Mistakes when Using Flashcards

In spite of the simplicity and popularity of flashcards, there are still many people who are guilty of using them ineffectively. Granted, there is no "wrong" way to use a flashcard. If it works, then it works. However, there are undeniably some best practices that most effectively promote efficiency in active recall when using flash cards. Here are some common mistakes that most people tend to make when incorporating flash cards into their study routines:

- Making flashcards that are only designed to induce rote learning.

- Creating flashcards that induce recognition instead of genuine recall.

- Making use of flashcards even when the subject matter requires a different approach

The Best Ways to Make Use of Flashcards

Studying while making use of flashcards is something that is a decision that you come to on your own. So, it would be foolish to try to impose all of these rules and guidelines on you if you feel like they won't really help you. However, it wouldn't hurt for you to open your mind up a little to the idea of using these trusted techniques to further your capacity to learn using flashcards.

Make your own flashcards from scratch

One basic rule of thumb for studying is that you should always deeply immerse yourself in the material that you are learning about as much as possible. This means that it would be much more effective for you to actually take the time to make your own flashcards from scratch instead of resorting to using someone else's flashcards for studying. The mental and emotional investment that you pour into creating your flashcards will definitely help in promoting critical thinking, understanding, and comprehension.

Incorporate images into your flashcards

If you are a more visual learner who is better stimulated by images and pictures, then don't be afraid of incorporating imagery into your flashcards. It's always encouraged that you get creative with the way that you design and structure your flashcards. Sometimes, making use of creative imagery can make an idea or a concept a lot more memorable and distinct.

Make use of mnemonic devices

The idea of mnemonic devices has already been explained in a previous chapter of this eBook. Don't be afraid to incorporate this study technique into your formation of flashcards as well. This is a prime example of being able to creatively incorporate two separate learning techniques into a single methodology.

Stick to one point per card

You don't want to overload your mind with flashcards. The whole point of flashcards as a methodology is to promote understanding through sheer repetition and genuine recall. It can be very hard to recall the information on a flashcard when it is filled with too many concepts and ideas. Stick to just one question and answer for every flashcard so that you don't end up overloading your senses.

Break down complicated ideas into multiple cards

Similar to the previous point on this list, it's important that you don't overload your senses with the amount of information that you put into a single card. That is why if you are faced with a difficult or challenging topic that is way too complex, it might be a good idea to break it down into separate questions fit for separate cards.

Talk out loud while studying

Even though you don't want to overload your senses while studying to the point where you compromise your capacity for comprehension, you are still going to want to recruit all of your senses in order to promote focus and concentration. That's why it really helps to say things out loud while your studying instead of just thinking about these ideas and concepts in your own mind. Making use of this technique can vastly aid in memorization and recall.

Study your flashcards in a non-linear fashion

It's likely that throughout the course of your study process, you aren't just going to be going through your flashcards in a single round. Flashcards are best used in accordance with the Spaced Repetition principle. But this is something that will be expanded on further in the next chapter. For now, you just want to make sure that when you do repeat your round of flashcards, you do so in a different order. Adding a sense of spontaneity in the way that you study your flashcards will enforce genuine recall as opposed to fake memorization and recognition.

Explore other methods of accelerated learning

Don't treat flashcards as if they're the only acceptable way to go about learning and studying. Yes, they can be very effective tools. However, just because this is a methodology that has proven its effectiveness in the past doesn't mean that it's always going to be effective in every single study situation that you find yourself in. In fact, flashcards can be used as a great supplement to other transformative learning methods. It's always nice when you are able to mix things up and see what works best for specific scenarios. That's why this eBook is such a great resource for you because you are afforded some other alternatives to accelerated learning which can be supplemented by other methods of studying. There is no one specific method that is going to work best for every single scenario.

Chapter 18: A Case for Spaced Repetition

What is the reason that you want to learn more about accelerated learning techniques in the first place? You want to save time. That's essentially the gist of your motivation, right? You value your time as a person, and always want to make the most of it. Unfortunately, traditional methods of studying are going to require a lot of time and effort, and they might not necessarily yield the most satisfactory results. You know that you have to devote x number of hours to studying a particular subject so that you can fully master it, but you only have so many hours in a day. This is essentially the problem that spaced repetition seeks to resolve.

Instead of studying for five hours straight in a single day, perhaps you should try studying for one hour each day for five days straight. You will notice that the latter method of studying is going to yield better results for you, and is going to be much easier to manage on your hectic schedule. This form of studying is precisely what you would call 'spaced repetition'. This chapter is going to touch upon why spaced repetition is such an effective mode of learning, and it's also going to delve deeper into how you can best maximize it to accelerate your own personal learning process.

How to Build a Sturdy Wall

Think of learning as you build a wall for a house with a pile of bricks. You first start with the base layer of bricks. You carefully cement each brick to the ground as you lay them next to one another until the entire first layer of the wall is complete. Then, you have to wait for the cement to solidify, and then you get to stacking the second layer of bricks on the wall. When you're done with that, you wait for the cement to solidify, and then you repeat the process until you're done with the entire facade.

Spaced repetition is essentially like building a brick wall. It's not just mindlessly stacking layers of bricks on top of one another without stopping. There are always going to have to be pauses in between in order to allow for the cement and bricks to settle and solidify themselves. That is exactly how the mind works. It would be very inefficient for you to try to process large amounts of information in an extended period of time without stopping. What you have to do is pace yourself properly. Consistent short bursts of learning and studying would be a lot better than a single marathon session of reading. That is essentially the gist behind the spaced repetition method of learning. It's not some long and drawn-out effort to build all four walls of a room in a single day. It's short and repetitive bursts of little efforts that you can give on a consistent basis in order to ensure the integrity of the room's foundation.

The Best Intervals for Spaced Repetition

You aren't merely content with understanding the idea of having to space out the study and learning sessions that you have. You want to know HOW you have to space them out. You want to get to the nitty-gritty aspects of it. As they say, the devil is in the details after all. You know that since scientists and researchers have proved the effectiveness of spaced repetition as a concept, then there must be optimal spacing intervals that people can partake in to maximize their learning. If you really do think that, then you would indeed be right. See how smart you are already? We haven't even finished this entire eBook yet.

It was Piotr Wozniak, the co-founder of learning and development software SuperMemo, that dedicated a bulk of his professional life to figuring out the ideal spacing intervals to maximize the positive effects of the spaced repetition methodology. It was his research in the field of spaced repetition that eventually led to him creating the algorithm that would later serve as the foundation for his SuperMemo learning software. We won't attempt to go in-depth on the ins and outs of his algorithm, but to give you a good sense of what his research suggested, this was what he found:

The first repetition should be performed after one day of the initial study session. The second repetition should occur 7 days after that. The third repetition should take place 16 days after that. And the final study repetition should take place 35 days after that.

And even though these are Wozniak's findings, you don't necessarily have to be so strict with following this specific format. Obviously, you can still adjust depending on your needs and personal goals. His research just offers you a better overview of how you would be able to structure your own repetition intervals as you embark on your path to learning.

Using Flashcards for Spaced Repetition

Remember how in the previous chapter, we talked about the usefulness and effectiveness of the traditional flashcard as a tool for learning? Well, there is a way to integrate the spaced repetition methodology into the flashcard method of learning in order to really optimize learning for both pedagogies. Granted, there are going to be several ways in which you would be able to execute your spaced repetition learning program with the use of flashcards. However, for the purposes of this eBook, we are going to focus on the simplest and easiest one to grasp: the Leitner system.

To understand how the Leitner system really works, imagine that you have prepared a set of flashcards that make up various questions and important points that are connected to the main topic that you need to study for an examination or a presentation. After preparing your flashcards, you will want to prepare around 5 different bundles or boxes. The number of boxes can vary depending on the amount of time that you have to prepare for a test or the number of flashcards that you might have. For the purpose of this example, let's say you have decided on 5 boxes.

To begin studying with the Leitner system, place all of the flashcards that you have into Box 1 and go through a round of testing. For every card in which you answer correctly, transfer the card into Box 2. Every card that you get wrong is going to have to remain in Box 1. This is a process that you will want to follow until you reach the fifth and final box. For every card that you get right, you have to graduate it onto the next box. However, for every card that you get wrong, you have to return it to Box 1 regardless of wherever that card was in the order of boxes when you got it wrong. Now that you understand the mechanics of the boxes and card transfers, it's now time to determine the proper spaced repetition intervals for the boxes.

Box 1 is a box that you will want to test yourself with every single day. Box 2 should be tested every other day. Box 3 should be tested once a week. Box 4 should be tested every four weeks. Lastly, Box 5 should be studied on the final week of exam preparations.

Alternative Platforms for Spaced Repetition

There are indeed plenty of platforms in which you would be able to apply the principle of spaced repetition. If you are using the flashcards, then you don't always have to use the Leitner system. If you're not interested in using flashcards altogether, then that would be fine as well. There is actually a whole bunch of software out there that is dedicated to helping people learn through the spaced repetition methodology. There are various apps that are available on Android, iOS, Windows, and Linux as well. It's all just a matter of you showing the willingness and initiative to explore and experiment a little bit. Part of learning is trying to figure out what method of learning works best for you.

Conclusion

At the end of the day, learning is always going to be a lifelong conquest. It's something that you are going to want to take seriously for as long as you live. The person who feels like they know everything is the person who is ultimately going to get left behind by those who accept that there is still much to learn in life. Allow your curiosities to drive and propel you forward. It's okay to come to terms with the fact that you don't know everything just yet. It's okay to admit to yourself that you are ignorant about something. Self-awareness is key to anyone's growth. The more aware you are of how much you don't know, the bigger your potential for knowledge and development is as a human being.

We all learn differently. Some of us learn with more visual aids, and some of us will prefer auditory aids. Some of us will manage to absorb an entire textbook's worth of knowledge within a day, and for some of us, it would take a little longer. It's all dependent on a human being's personality and approach to learning overall. But ultimately, the goals remain the same. It's all for the pursuit of knowledge, wisdom, and perspective. It's all about enhancing one's understanding of the world around them. It's really about expanding one's mind to be able to accommodate the vastness of information in the universe.

Learning is a process that you will need to undertake regardless of where you might be in life. During your formative years, you are forced to learn the basic principles and foundations of what it means to be a human being in this world. As you make your way through your schooling years, you are forced to learn topics that might be a little more complex but will help prepare you for adult life. Once you are starting out in your career, you are going to have to learn certain specialized concepts to help you get ahead in your field. When you are thinking of starting a family, you are going to have to learn the dynamics of raising a child and maintaining a household. Learning is a very personal journey that you embark upon until your time in this world is up.

It's already a given that the time that you have in this world is limited. Time is not something that can be borrowed, extended, or bargained for. That is why we must all make it a point to always make the most out of the time that we have in this world. If we waste our time with outdated, ineffective, and inefficient learning methods, then we are depriving ourselves of the time that we could be using to do other things in life such as engage in recreational activities or bond with the people that we love.

So, if you have an opportunity to improve and optimize the way that you approach learning, then you should always consider it at the very least. You always want to stay open to new ideas and new perspectives on how you can go about your daily processes, especially one that is as fundamental as learning. Accelerated learning offers you a chance to optimize the way that you gather, analyze, understand, and retain valuable information without having to demand too much of your time or energy. Life is multifaceted after all, and it should never be lived with just one facet being at the forefront all of the time. You don't always have to dedicate your *whole* life to serious learning and studying all of the time. But if you manage to integrate optimized learning methodologies in the way that you go about life as a whole, then it won't really have to feel like work at all. The best thing about accelerated learning methods is that they are designed to feel natural and organic. Once you are able to adopt a technique into the way that you analyze things, it becomes a part of who you are and how you approach new concepts and ideas.

Learning is not an endeavor that should only be reserved for the affluent, elite, and privileged overachievers of the world. Learning is something that everyone should always be able to have access to regardless of whatever one's background might be. With an abundance of accelerated learning techniques out there, it's near impossible for anyone to not be able to find one which would suit their own personal tastes, preferences, and goals.

Hopefully, this book will have provided valuable insight into the way you might approach learning and comprehension. You are a human being and you have dreams, and like everyone else, you have set goals for yourself. There are certain things in this life that you are looking to accomplish, and you] understand that the road to success is not paved to be easy. You know that there are plenty of things that you need to learn about for you to grow and prepare yourself for the challenges that are to come. You shouldn't let learning disabilities or inefficient learning methods keep you from your goals and dreams. Take advantage of the accelerated learning techniques that have been presented to you. You only have one life to live, and you want to make sure that you maximize it to the best of your abilities.

References

About A.L. (n.d.). Retrieved July 14, 2019, from https://www.alcenter.com/about-us/about-a-l/

AndersonSkylar, S. (2016, December 01). 7 Essential Steps to Cram for a Test Without Losing Your Mind. Retrieved from https://www.studyright.net/blog/7-essential-steps-to-cramming-for-exams-without-losing-your-mind/

Barker, E. (2015, May 11). How to Rapidly Accelerate Your Learning in 4 Easy Steps. Retrieved from https://observer.com/2015/05/how-to-rapidly-accelerate-your-learning-in-4-easy-steps/

Brown, E. (2017, June 07). 6 Advantages of Collaborative Learning. Retrieved from https://www.eztalks.com/online-education/advantages-of-collaborative-learning.html

Chaieb, L., Wilpert, E. C., Reber, T. P., & Fell, J. (2015, May 12). Auditory beat stimulation and its effects on cognition and mood States. Retrieved from https://www.ncbi.nlm.nih.gov/pmc/articles/PMC4428073/

Clark, B. (2015, March 23). Five Research-Backed Tips for Accelerated Learning. Retrieved from https://further.net/accelerated-learning/

Csadmin. (2017, December 27). New Infographic Exploring the Value of Study Buddies. Retrieved from https://www.careerstep.com/blog/career-step-publishes-a-new-infographic-on-the-value-of-study-buddies/

Effective Learning Program. (2010, April). The History of Accelerated Learning. Retrieved from http://effectivelearningprogram.blogspot.com/2010/04/accelerated-learning-is-model-of.html

Ferriss, T. (2019, May 28). Scientific Speed Reading: How to Read 300% Faster in 20 Minutes. Retrieved from https://tim.blog/2009/07/30/speed-reading-and-accelerated-learning/

Godman, H. (2018, April 05). Regular exercise changes the brain to improve memory, thinking skills. Retrieved from https://www.health.harvard.edu/blog/regular-exercise-changes-brain-improve-memory-thinking-skills-201404097110

Holdings, K. (2017, October 11). 8 Reasons Why Experiential Learning Is The Future Of Learning. Retrieved from https://elearningindustry.com/8-reasons-experiential-learning-future-learning

Learning Doorway. (n.d.). What Is Accelerated Learning? Retrieved July 14, 2019, from https://www.learningdoorway.com/accelerated-learning.html

Lee, D., & Hatesohl, D. (n.d.). Listening: Our Most

Used Communications Skill. Retrieved January 14, 2019, from https://extension2.missouri.edu/cm150

McCullough, J. (2013, September 01). The 5 Steps of Accelerated Learning. Retrieved from http://joe-mccullough.com/the-5-steps-of-accelerated-learning/

Mindvalley, Jon, Butcher, M., Fletcher, E., Walsch, N. D., Nichols, L., & Diamond, M. (2019, February 01). How To Study More Effectively Using Binaural Beats. Retrieved from https://blog.mindvalley.com/binaural-beats-for-study/

Nelson, B. (2012, July 30). Do You Read Fast Enough To Be Successful? Retrieved from https://www.forbes.com/sites/brettnelson/2012/06/04/do-you-read-fast-enough-to-be-successful/#7cfb6cf3462e

Oxford Learning. (2018, April 24). How To Take Study Notes: 5 Effective Note Taking Methods. Retrieved from https://www.oxfordlearning.com/5-effective-note-taking-methods/

Pierce, D. (2008). 10 Ways to Cram Successfully. Retrieved July 14, 2019, from http://www.gearfire.net/10-ways-cram-successfully/

Speedy Prep. (2013, November 12). 7 Benefits of Study Groups. Retrieved from https://www.speedyprep.com/blog/7-benefits-of-study-groups/

Talks, T. (2017, December 13). Want to learn better? Start mind mapping | Hazel Wagner | TEDxNaperville. Retrieved from https://www.youtube.com/watch?v=5nTuScU70As

Thomasfrank. (2018, November 20). 8 Better Ways to Make and Study Flash Cards. Retrieved from https://collegeinfogeek.com/flash-card-study-tips/

Thomasfrank. (2018, November 15). How to Remember More of What You Learn with Spaced Repetition. Retrieved from https://collegeinfogeek.com/spaced-repetition-memory-technique/

Watanabe-Crockett, L. (2018, January 06). A Path to Better Learning in the Age of Digital Distraction. Retrieved from https://www.wabisabilearning.com/blog/learning-age-digital-distraction

www.ingramcontent.com/pod-product-compliance
Lightning Source LLC
Chambersburg PA
CBHW071349080526
44587CB00017B/3031